THE 12 UNIVERSAL LAWS

Unleash the Secrets to Manifesting the Life of your Dreams NOW

Coco Faith

Copyright © 2023 by Coco Faith

All rights reserved.

No portion of this book may be reproduced in any form without written permission from the publisher or author, except as permitted by U.S. copyright law.

This publication is designed to provide accurate and authoritative information in regard to the subject matter covered. It is sold with the understanding that neither the author nor the publisher is engaged in rendering legal, investment, accounting or other professional services. While the publisher and author have used their best efforts in preparing this book, they make no representations or warranties with respect to the accuracy or completeness of the contents of this book and specifically disclaim any implied warranties of merchantability or fitness for a particular purpose. No warranty may be created or extended by sales representatives or written sales materials. The advice and strategies contained herein may not be suitable for your situation. You should consult with a professional when appropriate. Neither the publisher nor the author shall be liable for any loss of profit or any other commercial damages, including but not limited to special, incidental, consequential, personal, or other damages.

Book Cover by M A Rehman

1st Edition 2023

"The pain of not doing the work is far greater than the pain of doing the work. Because the work is where the breakthrough lives. The work is where the future is being created. The work is where you make a difference. It's where the meaning is. It's where the important stuff happens." **-Seth Godin**

Contents

INTRODUCTION	1
YOU ONLY LIVE ONCE	3
THE UNIVERSAL LAWS	5
1. THE LAW OF ONENESS	6
2. THE LAW OF VIBRATION	12
3. THE LAW OF INSPIRED ACTION	17
4. THE LAW OF CORRESPNDENCE	22
5. THE LAW OF ATTRACTION	27
6. THE LAW OF PERPETUAL TRANSMUTATON OF ENERGY	31
7. THE LAW OF CAUSE AND EFFECT	36
8. THE LAW OF COMPENSATION	41
9. THE LAW OF RELATIVITY	45
10. THE LAW OF POLARITY	50
11. THE LAW OF RHYTHM	55
12. THE LAW OF GENDER	59
13. LETTING GO	62
The Myth of the Perfect Time	63
You Have to Clear in Order to Create	67
Shedding Familial Limitations	70
Recognizing the Need for Change	74

Let the Universe Handle the How	77
The Open Hand Philosophy	81
The Light You Find in Your Darkest Hour	84
Healing the Soul through Ho'oponopono	87
When You Outgrow Your Tribe	89
14. GET CLEAR	92
Find Your North Star	93
Dream without Limits	97
The Power of Clear Intentions	100
Where Attention Flows, Energy Goes	103
Find Your Glimmers	107
Authenticity is the Highest Vibration	111
15. IT'S ALREADY MINE	115
Create Your Ultimate Vision Board	116
Who is Your Alter Ego?	121
Mantras as Manifestation Tools	125
Turning Envy into Inspiration	128
Visualization	133
Quantum Leaping Your Reality	136
16. REWIRE YOUR LIMITING BELIEFS	140
The Power of Your Subconscious Mind	141
Creating Your Reality With Words	143
The Hidden Benefits of Not Achieving	147
Flipping the Script	150
The Cords That Bind You	156
Lunar Magic	159

The Magic of "Thank You"	163
17. TAKE ALIGNED ACTION	166
Be Like Bamboo	167
The Voice that Whispers to You	170
18. LOOKING FOR GUIDANCE	174
Ask	175
Angel Numbers: The Universe's Secret Code	178
Akashic Records	181
What Rejection Teaches Us	184
The Power of Perseverance	187
Epilogue	191
Acknowledgments	192

INTRODUCTION

"Remember, Nothing Changes if Nothing Changes"
-John Rohn

LIFE'S JOURNEY OFTEN FEELS aimless, filled with struggle and self-doubt. Yet within each of us lies an inner wisdom that can guide our path if we learn to access it. What if I told you that by understanding 12 Universal Laws that shape our lives, we can tap into this wisdom and consciously create happier, more fulfilling lives?

These Universal Laws influence us, whether we realize it or not. They govern the growth of nature, societies, and our personal lives in ways we may not fully grasp. When we take the time to study them, a veil lifts. We begin to comprehend life's interconnectedness more deeply and how our thoughts, actions, and beliefs shape our reality.

Skeptical? Understandable. But suspend disbelief for a moment and imagine what might be possible. Picture yourself waking up with a clear sense of purpose, moving confidently toward meaningful goals. What could open up for you if you knew how to intentionally attract fulfilling relationships, abundant financial flow, and creativity into your life?

The 12 Laws provide a blueprint for conscious creation and living. As we align our inner world with these Laws, external reality organically shifts to reflect our empowered state back to us. We cease struggling upstream, instead moving with the currents of life in flow.

What might change for you if inner peace replaced self-judgment? If you faced life's ups and downs with equanimity rather than criticism? If you awakened to how your thoughts and behaviors have attracted past hardship, enabling you to blossom into your boldest self?

This book will explore the 12 Laws, revealing how to transform our lives by working with rather than against the invisible forces governing our world, both externally and from within. I invite you to begin your journey into conscious creation. A fulfilling life awaits you.

Note: For those with mental health conditions, please consult your healthcare provider before practising any new techniques.

Coco Faith

> "The universe depicted in this book can be adapted or interchanged to represent whatever belief system or perspective the reader holds. The author recognizes that readers come from many diverse backgrounds, faiths, and schools of thought that inform their understanding of existence and reality. As such, the cosmic realm portrayed here is not intended to promote any single philosophy but rather serve as a malleable landscape for readers to engage with. Readers are welcome and encouraged to conceptualize the universe within these pages in alignment with their personal truths, substituting terminology and interpretations to match their own understanding. This book aims to be an adaptable vehicle for readers to imbue with their own meaning and beliefs about the nature of reality."

YOU ONLY LIVE ONCE

WE ONLY GET ONE SHOT

L IFE IS A PRECIOUS gift that must not be taken for granted. We only get one shot at making the most of this world and leaving our mark. Yet, too often, we let worries, self-doubt or the busyness of life hold us back from truly living. We put off chasing dreams, taking risks, and engaging fully in each moment. But in postponing joy and purpose, we miss out on opportunities that may never come again.

Stop acting like you have infinite time. Our time here is fleeting. We must nurture our relationships, follow our passions, speak our truths, explore new horizons, and spread more light. The clock ticks; seasons change. Are we maximizing each day's potential or squandering this one chance at a meaningful existence?

MINDFULNESS LETS US FULLY ENGAGE

The key is living consciously through mindfulness, aware of our thoughts and intentions behind actions, big and small. Doing so lets us fully engage in every interaction and activity. We notice beauty everywhere and uncomplicate life by focusing only on this moment.

When we stop dwelling on the unchangeable past or unknowable future, we realize how precious 'now' is. Freed from overthinking, judging or trying to control things beyond our power, we access a natural state of peace, joy, and wisdom. We have space for creativity, connection, and living from the heart.

Love Fiercely

Knowing this life is our sole opportunity, we must love wholeheartedly, starting with ourselves. We are worthy; we matter. Our well-being enables us to uplift others, too. Forgiving imperfections, we build strong relationships by meeting people where they are, with openness, empathy, and support.

Despite hardship and heartbreak being inevitable, an undercurrent of love makes life's fullness — heights and depths — worthwhile. To limit regrets, we must communicate earnestly, reconcile willingly and part warmly. Gratitude and affection to those dearest to us sweeten each shared moment.

The Last Word Should Be Yours

Upon reaching life's end, you should have no apologies, excuses or explanations left to make. You should feel confident you held nothing back personally or professionally; you risked rejection and followed intuition over logic. Chasing purpose over status leaves you feeling fulfilled.

Ultimately, you alone craft your legacy with vision, values, and victories that define success on your terms. You gain satisfaction from whatever time remains by appreciating everything and remembering that today, well lived, leads to no regrets tomorrow. Our one life warrants full engagement while we have the chance. What dreams will you make reality starting today?

THE UNIVERSAL LAWS

Chapter 1

THE LAW OF ONENESS

"When we realize we are connected to everyone and everything in the universe, we realize there is no such thing as others. There is only us." **-Abraham Hicks**

> **The Law**
>
> **The Law of Oneness** states that we are all interconnected as part of the same universal energy force. Though appearing separate, there is an underlying field of unity beneath the diversity of all life. Science reveals that at a quantum level, everything is composed of the same subatomic particles and waves of energy. We are all expressions of the same universal consciousness. When we have insights of oneness, we naturally treat all life with compassion, knowing we are all reflections of each other.

A Moment of Connection

The crash of the waves filled my ears with a rhythmic roar as I gazed out into the vast ocean. At 13 years old, alone on the beach, I was blanketed in stillness—a tranquility so deep it seeped into my bones. I wandered onto the sandy shore, shells crunching underfoot, as a sense of profound unity washed over me. I felt intricately woven into the tapestry of nature surrounding me; the swirling tides, the crying gulls dancing on the breeze, the vibration of life embedded into each tiny shell fragment.

I was but a strand in a greater web, individual yet connected to everything. In that moment, something deep within me resonated with the wisdom of interbeing—the innate interconnectedness of all living things. This wisdom pointed to an ancient truth: that all of life is one, that separateness is but an illusion. While I did not have the words as a child, the feeling imprinted onto my soul. I breathed in the vision of the ocean as my vision breathed into me. Two fragments of the same wholeness dancing together. Whenever I lost my way, this remembered feeling would come flooding back like the inevitable tide, reminding me I belonged.

The Threads that Bind Us

Oneness means that deep down within us, there is no separation. We are all tiny drops of water in a great cosmic ocean. Seen from the surface, each drop appears separate and distinct. But underneath it all flows in one tremendous river of energy and consciousness that connects us all.

When we can tap into this quantum realm of oneness, we gain access to unlimited collective power - the power of unity, harmony, and love. We realize we're never alone on this journey of life. Wherever we are, there are threads tying us together with the rest of humanity and all living beings.

Understanding that everything emanates from the same source is transformative because it shifts our entire perception of the world. Suddenly the lines that seem to divide us dissolve away. Oneness means that deep down, there's no **"other."**

The same universal consciousness that flows through me also flows through you, through all of our neighbors here on this planet, and through every tree, bird, and living creature on Earth. We're all tiny cells in the greater body of life.

What Oneness Means for Our World

This perspective naturally gives rise to greater empathy, compassion, and care - not just for other people, but for our shared world. When we hurt others, we indirectly hurt ourselves by damaging the collective whole. But likewise, when we help others, we help the larger tapestry of life.

Oneness reminds us that we're all swimming together in the same current, all traveling downstream together in the same direction. By remembering this unity instead of only seeing division, we begin to align our actions with the quantum field of infinite potential.

We become better conduits for manifestations that benefit the whole rather than just ourselves. **Everything we think, say, and do sends ripples through the entire web of life.**

Flashes of Interconnection

We've all likely had moments when we felt strangely linked to those around us—hints that we're all connected:

- You think of someone you haven't spoken to in ages when your phone lights up with their name.

- An urge to check in on a friend in need hits you an hour before their distressed call comes through.

- While sitting quietly by the ocean, you sense your place within the whole—the crashing waves, crying gulls, scuttling crabs all feel intricately linked as one coordinated dance, and you with them. You feel at one with it all.

- Making eye contact with a stranger passing by, you recognize a profound kinship in that brief shared moment of humanity. Their hopes, struggles, and purpose all reflected in eyes that mirror your own.

These flashes pierce the illusion of separateness. Like glitches in the matrix, they reveal an underlying fabric of togetherness—a single consciousness expressed through an infinite diversity of form. When we notice these signs, we realign with the wisdom of interconnection that lives inside each of us.

These synchronicities remind us that beneath the physical world we can see and touch, there is another realm that connects us all. Quantum physicists have found a similar effect between subatomic particles called **"quantum entanglement."** Even when separated by distance, particles instantaneously influence each other, as if exchanging information through an invisible universal energy field.

This phenomenon confirms what ancient spiritual traditions have told us since the beginning of time - at a fundamental level, everything and everyone is interconnected through a vast quantum web of oneness.

Harnessing Our Collective Power

Since we're all connected, we can accelerate positive change by combining our energy and intention with others. Just as two candle flames grow stronger when united, we can multiply the power of our focused intentions through collective unity.

Ways we can tap into this potent combined energy:

- **Intention circles:** A group sits in a circle taking turns sharing dreams and goals. Together the group then visualizes each person's desires realized. This shared visualization field creates faster manifestation results.

- **Volunteer initiatives:** When people unite through compassionate service to uplift their community, they align with humanity's core aspiration of caring for one another. This builds our co-creative abilities.

- **Support communities:** By sharing personal dreams and struggles, groups create encouragement, inspiration and clarity. Getting feedback helps refine ideas while aligning intentions.

In each case, the goal is empowering each other through recognizing our innate connection.

By consciously combining our creative energy, we can achieve goals and create change that is not possible alone. Our collective potential is great when we harmonize as one.

Living the Lessons Daily

While fleeting spiritual epiphanies can fuel us, integrating oneness into our day-to-day lives is where real transformation unfolds through sustained practice. Start with these simple ways:

- Begin each morning by sending loving kindness to strangers and friends alike. See all as united.

- When making choices, reflect on how even small actions send ripples through our collective whole.

- Spend meditative time in nature observing the interconnected web of life. Know you are part of this tapestry.

- Share dreams with loved ones. Listen sincerely to theirs. Support each other's growth.

- Find volunteer work benefiting your wider community. Help humanity move forward together.

These practical first steps nurture awareness of an awakening truth:

> **Our shared connection is real and ever-present in every moment.**

As this unity consciousness takes deeper root through daily practice, relationships and communities will organically transform from the inside-out. Live from this place of oneness even during struggles. Meet conflict with empathy by seeing the light within all.

As we delve deeper into the tapestry of interconnectedness, we unravel the profound implications of this universal truth. The Law of Oneness beckons us not only to understand but to embody this principle in our daily lives. Each sunrise offers an invitation to embrace the unity that binds us all. Through every action and interaction, we have the power to honor this connection. By extending kindness, fostering empathy, and nurturing collective well-being, we participate in the symphony of existence, harmonizing our individual melodies into a grander, more resonant chorus. As we walk this path of unity, let us not merely tread lightly but leave imprints of compassion, weaving a world where the threads of interconnection are cherished and celebrated.

When thoughts, words and actions align into harmony, we quicken the blossoming of our collective potential. May we walk this path with open hands, open hearts, and deepening trust in the truth that we are all one.

Chapter 2

THE LAW OF VIBRATION

"Everything in the Universe has a certain vibrational frequency. By projecting frequencies of health, joy and love, you can change your world." - **Eileen Anglin**

THE LAW

The Law of Vibration states that everything in the universe is energy and vibrates at its own unique frequency. Our feelings, thoughts, and beliefs emit vibrational frequencies that attract corresponding experiences. When our dominant vibrations align with what we desire, we manifest those outcomes. By raising our vibration through positive thoughts, affirmations, visualization, and other uplifting practices, we can tune into higher frequencies and attract abundant outcomes. Lower vibrations of fear, doubt, and negativity conversely attract unwanted conditions. Consciously regulating vibration is key to manifesting. We shape our reality through the energy we radiate.

Have you ever walked into a room and immediately sensed a dramatic energy shift that left you feeling uplifted or drained? Instinctively we read and respond to vibrational frequencies around and within us. Like music, each of us projects a unique energy field that touches all those we come into contact with. Our vibration impacts the world.

Everything in the universe, including you, vibrates at its specific frequency. Essentially, vibration is energy that resonates on higher and lower frequencies. The Law of Vibration reveals that by consciously raising your personal energy vibration, you attract more positive experiences. Lower vibrations align you with increased negativity and challenges.

> **Put simply, your vibe attracts your tribe.**

Through practices like exercise, spending time in nature, and meditation, you can skillfully attune yourself to higher frequencies of harmony and flow. But first, what does it feel like when your vibration is elevated?

What High Vibrations Feel Like

Imagine for a moment you've just gotten engaged to the love of your life. Joy radiates through your entire being as you make wedding plans and envision your happy future together. Anything seems possible. The feeling of profound connectedness, purpose, and optimism overflows in your heart. This emotional experience reflects heightened energy vibrations within and around you. When you personally attune with heartfelt desires in this way, even briefly, you generate immense magnetic power to draw them into your reality over time.

Your Dominant Vibration

Now, realistically, no one can remain on a continuous emotional high at all times. Humans experience a vast range of feelings, from sadness to elation. But what matters most is your dominant vibration over time. When higher frequency energies of love, peace and purpose prevail in your being over weeks and months, you become exponentially more receptive to expanded blessings and synchronicities flowing into your life. Even when facing inevitable challenges that trigger lower emotions, see them as opportunities to rediscover inner stillness and balance. With practice, consciously return your focus to the positive by applying energy-clearing and elevating techniques that resonate most. As your dominant vibration lifts, your outside world has no choice but to transform to match your new energy field.

> "If you want to find the secrets of the universe, think in terms of energy, frequency, and vibration." -**Nikola Tesla**

WHAT RADIO STATION ARE YOU LISTENING TO?

Think of vibration like a radio station. At any moment, you are tuned to a station - it could be playing uplifting, inspiring music...or heavy static.

Through unconscious limiting habits and reactions, your inner radio may currently carry frequencies generating feelings like scarcity, anxiety, and negativity. This station sounds disjointed. It drains you while keeping life stuck on repeat.

But you have the power to change the dial to tune into an energizing station. This higher vibe station plays frequencies, creating emotions of creativity, joy, purpose, and abundance. By consciously shifting your inner vibration, everything in your outer world begins to shift and align with this positive energy.

SIGNS YOU ARE IN A HIGH VIBE STATE:

- Boundless energy, vitality, enthusiasm, feeling connected to soul purpose, lightness, playfulness, not bothered by drama, confidence in self-expression, taking inspired action, noticing beauty all around, animals and children gravitate to you and feeling compassion for all.

When vibration is raised, you shine as your best, most vibrant self. Others will notice and be drawn to your light. Be the energy that no matter where you go, you always add value.

Signs You Are In A Low Vibe State:

- Feeling drained, fatigued, lacking motivation, disconnected from purpose, questioning life path, heaviness, difficulty feeling light or playful, caught up in or triggered by drama, doubt or hesitation in expressing oneself, stuckness, struggling to take action, boredom, overlooking beauty, noticing lack, judging self or others, lacking compassion, drinking too much and gossiping.

When vibration is lowered, it can be challenging to shine as your best self. Others may pick up on the low energy. Bring awareness to where you are right now without judgment. Even the darkest nights contain seeds of growth.

Focus first on nourishing and filling up your cup. Small acts of self-care and saying "no" to energy drains can go a long way. When ready, look for simple ways to lift your vibe - a walk in nature, an uplifting chat with a friend, or listening to an inspiring podcast.

Rather than striving, be gentle with yourself as you raise your frequency bit by bit. Meet yourself where you're at while remaining open to receiving guidance on the next steps toward the light.

How does this work exactly?

The universe is pure energy vibrating at different frequencies. Like attracts like. When your dominant energy vibration rises to match the positive frequency of your desired dreams and goals, you draw those uplifted outcomes seamlessly into your life.

For example, focusing daily on feeling abundant joy and gratitude now energetically summons more reasons to feel grateful. The high vibe emotions signal creation to send you more joy-filled experiences. The key is consciously envisioning your dream as if it's arrived while injecting higher frequencies into each day through simple, uplifting practices. As you raise your energy setpoint, the extraordinary becomes the norm. Things once seen as miracles manifest as everyday life.

While cultivating patience for desires unfolding in perfect timing, know that the quantum universe already contains in potential what you wish to attract. Aligning your vibration simply allows you to tune into and thereby experience more uplifting realities already existing all around you.

> **Be the energy that no matter where you go, you always add value.**

In understanding the Law of Vibration, we embark on an empowering journey of self-awareness and intentional living. Our emotions, thoughts, and actions emit frequencies that harmonize with the energies surrounding us. We are, in essence, tuning forks capable of aligning with varying frequencies. Picture this: each interaction, decision, and emotion as a dial adjusting the resonance of your personal frequency. Recognizing where we stand on this spectrum allows us to fine-tune our vibrational output consciously. When we consciously choose the frequency we wish to broadcast, we exert a tremendous influence on the experiences and circumstances that unfold in our lives. It's a dance of energies where our inner state becomes the composer of our reality, orchestrating a symphony of experiences that resonate with our chosen vibrations.

Chapter 3

THE LAW OF INSPIRED ACTION

"Be not afraid of going slowly; be only afraid of standing still."
-Chinese Proverb

THE LAW

The Law of Inspired Action means following intuition and synchronicity to achieve your desires rather than forcing outcomes. Once you set a clear intention, ideas and opportunities will arise naturally to guide you effortlessly toward your goal. Pay attention to signs from the universe nudging you forward. Take actions that light you up, even if the path seems unconventional. Have faith that everything is unfolding for you perfectly. Don't try to rush or control the process. Trust in the universal timing. By acting from inspiration rather than pure effort, you open yourself up to receive support and resources to flow through you.

COCO FAITH

HAVE YOU EVER HELD A DREAM BUT STRUGGLED TO TAKE STEPS TO MAKE IT REAL?

OR PERHAPS THEY STARTED out enthusiastically but ran into resistance and fear? We all face challenges in bridging the gap between our desires and seeing them come alive. Sometimes the hardest truth is there isn't a villain out to get you, sometimes your worst enemy is you.

Inspired action is the bridge that allows us to cross from visualizing our goals to experiencing them. While positive intention-setting is crucial, we must also move our feet toward our dreams to make them real. When we direct our energy toward our desires through action aligned with purpose, we propel our lives in incredible new directions. We unlock our greatest potential. Milestones that once seemed impossible draw closer each time we act on an inspired impulse.

I will never forget a pivotal night years ago when I took a leap of inspired action that altered my entire life's trajectory...

It was 11:55 p.m., and the deadline to enter the grand prize newspaper contest loomed. I was still one newspaper token short. As the clock ticked down, I felt a sudden urge to act. I raced into the darkness, digging through recycling bins until—at last—the final glimmering token!

A few weeks later came the shocking call that, out of thousands of entries, I'd won a week of luxury prizes. Even more life-changing, the prize money provided the funds to pay off all my debts and purchase my first home. The dream of standing debt-free in my own home had become a reality, all because I listened to that voice in my head and took inspired action.

When inspiration strikes, we must silence our doubts and act on it with conviction. By taking aligned action on that midnight impulse, I manifested my desire. You can, too.

Aligning with the Flow

Inspired action isn't solely about hard work and self-discipline, as vital as they are. Equally important is aligning with the natural flow so the universe can work through you and with you. We must be willing to allow our desires to ebb and flow. Be open to receiving your goals in unexpected ways or timing if we cling too tightly to the how and when we constrict the creative potential of the universe.

When we're tuned into this higher flow, we gain intuitive clarity about our next step. Opportunities seem to serendipitously arise, resources align at just the right time, and obstacles dissolve. There's a sense of effortless magic.

We know we're in alignment when we receive intuitive nudges guiding our choices and experience chance encounters leading to major breakthroughs. A deep sense of trust replaces fear and doubt. Sometimes, getting out of your own way is the wisest action of all. By aligning with the natural flow, desired outcomes are drawn to you effortlessly.

Be water, not stone.

Moving Through Resistance

When inspired action feels uncertain or uncomfortable, limiting beliefs often arise, like **"I'm not ready yet"** or **"What if I fail?"** We've all been there!

By acknowledging these resistances with compassion and then reconnecting to our inner wisdom and strength, we can move through whatever blocks us. Our growth depends on moving through barriers.

STARTING SMALL

Inspired action often begins with small steps in the right direction. Each step builds unstoppable momentum.

We can break big goals into daily bite-sized actions. Focusing on progress, not perfection, keeps motivation high. Celebrate forward movement, no matter how small! When the universe sees us doing our part, it meets us more than halfway. Our steady efforts compound into major results over time.

> "Don't wait until everything is just right. It will never be perfect. There will always be challenges, obstacles, and less-than-perfect conditions. So what. Get started now. With each step you take, you will grow stronger." **Mark Victor Hansen**

MORE TIPS FOR APPLYING INSPIRED ACTION

- Start with small, consistent steps in the right direction. Each one builds momentum. Celebrate all progress.

- Trust perfect timing. Results sometimes take time to blossom. Stay persistent in following intuitive nudges. Appreciate each phase of your journey.

- Break big goals into daily bite-sized actions. Focus on progress over perfection. Tracking incremental wins keeps motivation high.

- Notice **"coincidences"** as signs you're aligned. Chance encounters and synchronicities show the universe is supporting you.

- When you feel resistance, reconnect to your vision to regain motivation. Believe in your inner wisdom and strength to succeed.

Taking inspired action aligned with your intentions allows you to build the bridge from dreams into reality. You have all you need within. Progress starts with a single step.

BRIDGING THE GAP THROUGH INSPIRED ACTION

The Law of Inspired Action reminds us that aligned action is the vessel through which our desires manifest. When inspiration strikes, we must act on it decisively and with full commitment. Inspired action propels our lives in incredible new directions, unlocking our greatest potential. It is not enough to merely envision our goals - we must bridge the gap between visualizing and experiencing through mindful, purposeful action. Though obstacles will inevitably arise, by moving through resistance with faith and perseverance, we draw closer to our dreams each time we act. When we combine inspired action with trust in divine timing, desired outcomes will blossom. If we wish to see our intentions realized, we must be willing to silence the inner critic, move through fear, start small, and build unstoppable momentum, for it is action alone that allows us to fully bridge the gap from imagination to creation.

Chapter 4

THE LAW OF CORRESPNDENCE

"As within, so without; as above, so below; as the universe, so the soul" - **Hermes Trismegistus**

THE LAW

The Law of Correspondence states that what is within is reflected without. Our **outer world mirrors our inner state**. By transforming our conscious and subconscious beliefs, emotions, and energy, we transform what we experience externally. This law highlights the power of our inner world to shape outer reality. When we heal inner wounds, external relationships and circumstances heal, too. Similarly, to change negative patterns, we must address the root causes inside. The law applies across scales as well; the microcosm reflects the macrocosm.

THE INTIMATE DANCE BETWEEN WITHIN AND WITHOUT

Have you ever noticed how your external world seems to mirror your internal state? When you feel clear, calm, and focused inside, your outside life tends to flow more smoothly. But when your inner world is chaotic or turbulent, your external reality reflects that.

Demystifying the Microcosm and Macrocosm

The Law of Correspondence is encapsulated in the ancient Hermetic saying, **"As above, so below; as below, so above."** This means the visible patterns and rhythms we observe "above" in the celestial spheres and unseen universe also exist "below" in the realm of our individual lives.

The macrocosm represents the vast scale of the cosmos, encompassing stars, galaxies, dark matter, and the universal forces governing it all. The microcosm signifies our human experience—our individual thoughts, choices, relationships, and lives.

At first glance, these realms appear totally separate. But in fact, they are intricately interconnected. The Law of Correspondence reveals the hidden unity between **"above"** and **"below."**

Consider how the cells in our bodies divide, grow, and die in cycles and rhythms that mirror the celestial cycles of solar systems and galaxies being born and dissolving. The firing of neurons in our brains is echoed in the flashing synapses of lightning storms. Even the structure of the atom, with its central nucleus orbited by electrons, resembles the configuration of our solar system, with the sun encircled by planets.

> "Outer changes always begin within." **-Byron Katie**

The Unity of Microcosm and Macrocosm

This law reminds us that we are both the microcosm and the macrocosm. Within each of us exists the whole of the universe. We each contain a unique spark of the Divine, making us each infinitely powerful creators. Yet we are also part of the greater Cosmos - tiny replicas of the immense.

When we look inward, we find the outer mirrored back to us. Our innermost essence reflects the absolute, and the dance of our lives rhymes with the rhythms of galaxies being born. In stillness, we may hear the music of the spheres and know ourselves as microcosms of the macrocosm - individual notes in the grand cosmic symphony. Our inner harmony brings outer harmony.

Dancing Between Opposites

It also teaches that balance and harmony are not static blissful states but a dynamic dance between opposites. Light exists only in contrast to darkness. True relaxation can only be appreciated after exertion and effort. We cannot experience the joy of reunion without temporary separation.

Restful play and quiet solitude serve as a counterbalance to periods of intense creative work or social activity in your own life. Challenges organically lead to growth and renewal. Trust in these natural cycles rather than resisting change. The flow between opposites to maintain energetic harmony.

When external situations try to pull you out of balance, retreat inward. Replenish your spirit with activities and experiences you love, like reading an inspiring book, taking a bath, or having a movie night with family. Keep your inner world well-nourished and centred, no matter what storms might be brewing outside. From this place of calm, you can gracefully continue dancing through life's endless ups and downs.

Integrating Inner and Outer Awareness

To fully harness the Law of Correspondence, we must recognize that our inner and outer realities engage in a symbiotic dance, continuously impacting each other. For example, spending time in nature can shift our energy and perspective, leading to breakthrough ideas and changes in external habits. Likewise, adopting a new exercise routine or diet may transform our mental state or energy levels, rippling into other areas of life.

Make a habit of checking in with yourself daily. How is my inner world today? And how might that be shaping my outer experiences? By cultivating this inner-outer awareness, you become the master of your reality. You can spot imbalances early and make adjustments. This integration allows you to consciously create instead of feeling like life is happening to you.

Setting intentions with mindfulness

Intention-setting and mindfulness are powerful tools for harnessing the Law of Correspondence. When you set clear intentions for your desired outcomes, you align your inner world with what you wish to manifest externally. Combining this practice with present-moment mindfulness enables you to discern whether your thoughts, words, and actions are in harmony with your stated intentions and higher purpose.

For example, you may set an intention to attract a new romantic relationship, but subconsciously limiting beliefs around your worthiness could be misaligning you energetically. Through mindfulness, you can catch those self-sabotaging thoughts and work to replace them with empowering beliefs aligned with love. In this way, intention-setting combined with mindfulness helps ensure you are sending coherent signals internally and externally.

Mastering the Inner World

To truly harness the Law of Correspondence, we must recognize that our inner world is the realm of cause, while the outer world is the realm of effect. When our thoughts, words, and actions align internally, our external reality organically transforms as a result.

For example, limiting beliefs create energetic blockages that prevent us from manifesting our dreams. If you constantly think to yourself, "I struggle to make ends meet," you continually experience financial lack. But do the inner work of shifting this scarcity mindset, and your outer circumstances will shift too.

Of course, we cannot control everything that happens externally at all times. But we have full dominion over our inner domain—our thoughts, beliefs, emotions, perceptions, and intentions. This is where our real creative power lies. We can mindfully choose inner patterns that serve our highest good instead of being dominated by outdated negative programs on autopilot.

Surrendering to the Flow

Surrendering does not mean passive resignation but rather embodying a deep trust in the wisdom of each moment. When you embrace arising circumstances and opportunities rather than forcing a set outcome, you align yourself with the cosmic currents of the macrocosm. You loosen the ego's grip and let your highest self step into the flow.

This process is akin to a traveler encountering a fork in the road. Rather than rigidly committing to one direction, you feel out the energies of each path. By opening your mind and listening to your intuition, insights arise as to the right way forward. Your role becomes simply to feel, reflect, and take the next organic step.

Practically, this means not resisting when life takes you on an unexpected detour. Release your attachment to rigid plans and be open to improvisation. Let go of fears about the future. Respond to each moment afresh rather than being constrained by past patterns.

Chapter 5

THE LAW OF ATTRACTION

"You are what you think about." –**Dr. Robert Schuller**

> **The Law**
>
> The Law of Attraction is the principle that we attract whatever we focus on most. Our dominant thoughts, beliefs, and feelings act as an energetic magnet, drawing matching experiences into our lives. This law works through vibration. We radiate out frequencies that align with our inner state. Positive energy attracts positive outcomes, while negative energy attracts negatives.

Manifesting Your Dreams Using the Law of Attraction

Have you ever intensely desired something, yet despite your efforts, it remained out of reach? Or have you unexpectedly attracted an amazing opportunity that seemed magically aligned with your wishes?

Most of us have experienced manifestations like these, reflecting the hidden forces shaping our lives. Understanding the potent Law of Attraction helps unlock the mystery of why some dreams materialize easily while others stay trapped in our minds.

The Law of Attraction reveals that, energetically, you are the creator of your reality. You can consciously manifest your deepest intentions through your thoughts, emotions, beliefs, and actions. Mastering this law can profoundly transform your existence once you comprehend how it works.

This law states that your predominant thoughts and feelings emit frequencies that attract matching circumstances and experiences. Like a magnet, you draw more of whatever energy you habitually broadcast through your beliefs, imagination, and mental focus.

By intentionally directing your inner world, you directly shape your outer world. If you chronically fixate on problems or lack thereof, you attract more of those struggles. But if you consistently visualize success and radiate positive emotions, you summon more of those joyful experiences.

Taking Control of Your Manifestations

You now hold the keys to consciously creating your reality. By directing your predominant thoughts, emotions, beliefs, imagination, and actions towards your deepest desires, you activate this universal law. Monitor your inner world, releasing limiting programs and cultivating empowering beliefs. With consistency and passion, broadcast your intentions through visualizations, affirmations, inspired action and gratitude. You are the master of your energy and magnetism. Keep your frequency tuned to your dreams, and with focus and faith, you will attract their manifestation. This is your birthright - to consciously shape your existence through the magnetic power within. Master your mindset and energy, and any dream you can conceive is yours to achieve.

Thoughts and Feelings Shape Your World

Your thoughts and emotions generate the vibrational frequencies that largely steer what you attract. By directing them consciously, you take the reins of your results.

Thoughts are the building blocks of your existence. Whatever occupies your mind consistently expands in your world. Maintaining focus on your desires through tools like visualization, affirmations, journaling, and dominion over your mindset triggers the Law of Attraction to deliver more aligned opportunities. This explains the immense power of sustained, intentional thought.

Emotions indicate how energetically aligned you are with your dreams. Feelings like joy, excitement, passion, and enthusiasm emit high-vibrational frequencies that summon your goals into physical form. Negative emotions like fear, anxiety, doubt, and anger emit the opposite signal. Monitor your emotions as feedback for adjusting your focus and continually attracting your aspirations rather than your worries.

When your predominant thoughts, emotions, imagination, and actions stay fixed on your intentions, you transmit a steady frequency out to the universe that activates the Law of Attraction. Aligned circumstances, resources, and people then converge to help your desires manifest.

You decide you want a black Range Rover, so you start spotting them everywhere as your mind tunes in and looks out for them. It's the same with opportunities - if you open your mind to possibilities, you will start seeing opportunities everywhere, as if a door has opened. So walk on through!

Manifesting Using Gratitude and Acceptance

An essential component of consciously utilizing the Law of Attraction is cultivating profound gratitude for your current life while accepting where you are on your path. Gratitude energizes and magnetizes, attracting more of what you appreciate. When you acknowledge the blessings in your life right now instead of fixating on what is missing, you signal to the universe your readiness to receive abundance. Acceptance of your present reality as part of your growth journey diffuses resistance blocking your manifestations. By blessing your life in this moment, you allow your intentions to unfold organically rather than forcing them. Gratitude and acceptance create internal harmony that mirrors the circumstances you wish to attract. Make it a daily practice to find things to appreciate in both your challenges and blessings. This mental approach keeps you energized, optimistic and aligned with the fulfillment of your deepest desires.

The Power of Your Subconscious Mind

Your subconscious beliefs, assumptions, and programs also strongly influence your ability to manifest intentionally using the Law of Attraction. These ingrained mental patterns operate below your conscious awareness yet profoundly shape what you believe is possible. Your subconscious mind is the fertile foundation on which your outer life experiences are constructed.

> "Your subconscious mind grows either flowers or weeds in the garden of your life, whichever you plant with the mental equivalents you create." **– Joseph Murphy**

When your conscious desires align with your subconscious assumptions and programming, you can effectively manifest your goals using the Law of Attraction. However, if your conscious intentions contradict limiting subconscious beliefs, those beliefs usually dominate and obstruct your manifestations.

With awareness and patience, techniques like inner child work, tapping, and visualization can help transform restrictive subconscious programs and align them with your goals. While this takes consistent effort, expanding your self-concept and beliefs ultimately allows you to wield this law consciously and powerfully.

The Law of Attraction provides an empowering opportunity to shape your life according to your truest desires and higher purpose. Commit fully while embracing the journey with optimism. With focused belief and inspired action, you can manifest your dreams.

Chapter 6

THE LAW OF PERPETUAL TRANSMUTATON OF ENERGY

"We cannot destroy energy, we can only transform it from one manifestation into another" – **Nikola Tesla**

THE LAW

The Law of Perpetual Transmutation of Energy states that all energy is in a constant state of motion and transformation. Energy cannot be destroyed or cease to exist; it only shifts from one form to another. Our thoughts and emotions emit energy that takes on creative form. By transfusing our energy with positive intentions, we transform our outer world. Anger transmutes into calm through mindfulness and fear into courage through action. This law empowers us to deliberately direct energy towards desired change. Though energies may appear positive or negative, their purpose is transformation.

THE POWER TO CHANGE

THE PILE OF OLD Legos gathering dust in my bedroom held no joy for 8-year-old me. But with focused creativity, I transformed the dusty bricks into a majestic castle. This illustrates the Law of Perpetual

Transmutation of Energy—the principle that energy is constantly changing form. At any moment, we can direct energy transformation towards growth and positive change.

Like me building my Lego castle, we all have untapped creative power within us and often overlook opportunities for harnessing this energy. Through intention and imagination, we can shift stagnant energy into dynamic new expressions. The Law of Perpetual Transmutation teaches us that change is the only constant. Rather than remaining stuck in negative patterns, we can consciously channel our energy to improve anything in our lives.

Observe where energy feels blocked or dormant in your own life now. Examine limiting beliefs and attitudes that resist growth and perpetuate the status quo. Then set your intention to transform that energy. Dream boldly about how to shape that energy into uplifting new forms. Keep taking steps, no matter how small, to turn those intentions into reality. Like my dusty Lego bricks, every seemingly stuck situation contains the seeds of transformation.

The Flow of Energy

At the heart of the Law of Perpetual Transmutation of Energy is the idea that energy is always flowing and changing form. This energy can be physical, emotional, mental, or spiritual. It can manifest as thoughts, emotions, actions, and intentions. Nothing in the universe remains static; all is in a state of perpetual motion.

Consider the example of water. It can exist in various forms—solid as ice, liquid as water, or gas as steam—depending on the temperature. Similarly, the energy within us and around us is constantly shifting and evolving, responding to the conditions and vibrations of the moment.

HARNESSING THE FLOW

To harness the power of this law, it is essential to understand that we have the ability to influence the direction and quality of energy. Just as a dam controls the flow of water, our thoughts, intentions, and actions direct the flow of energy in our lives.

When we focus our energy on positive thoughts, intentions, and actions, we encourage the transmutation of energy into higher, more beneficial forms. Conversely, dwelling on negative thoughts or actions can lead to the transmutation of energy into lower, less desirable forms.

THE ROLE OF CONSCIOUSNESS

Consciousness plays a central role in the law of transmutation. Our awareness of the energy within and around us enables us to make conscious choices about how we direct and utilize that energy.

Through self-awareness and mindfulness, we can become attuned to the quality of our thoughts and emotions. We can recognize when our energy is flowing in a direction that aligns with our desires and values and when it does not. This awareness empowers us to make conscious shifts in our thoughts and intentions.

THE CREATIVE PROCESS

The law is closely tied to the creative process. When we harness it effectively, we become active participants in the creative unfolding of our lives.

The process begins with a clear vision or intention. We set our sights on what we wish to create or manifest. This vision acts as a powerful magnet, drawing the energy and resources needed to bring it into reality.

As we hold this vision, our thoughts, emotions, and actions align with it, transmuting energy into forms that support our goal. This alignment attracts opportunities, people, and circumstances that are in harmony with our vision, ultimately leading to its realization.

Transforming Negativity

The Law of Transmutation empowers us to convert lower vibrational energies into higher ones. It recognizes that negativity is a natural part of life but also that we possess the capacity to transform it. By consciously choosing to focus on positive thoughts and emotions, we can transmute negativity into positivity.

This law encourages us to face challenges with resilience and optimism, knowing that we have the power to change our circumstances through the energy we project. When we understand the potential for transformation, even the most daunting obstacles become opportunities for growth and manifestation.

Letting Go of Resistance

One of the challenges in working with this law is recognizing and releasing resistance to change. Resistance can take the form of doubts, fears, limiting beliefs, or attachments to the status quo. When we resist change, we impede the natural flow of energy and hinder its transmutation into higher forms.

To overcome resistance, it's important to cultivate trust and surrender. Trust in the natural order of the universe and in your ability to navigate change. Surrender to the flow of energy, allowing it to carry you toward growth and transformation.

Embracing Change

Change is often met with resistance because it can be uncomfortable and challenging. However, when we recognize that change is the vehicle for growth and improvement, we can approach it with greater openness and acceptance.

By consciously directing our energy toward positive change and personal development, we become co-creators of our own evolution. We can transmute lower vibrational energy—such as fear, doubt, or stagnation—into higher forms of energy—such as courage, confidence, and creativity.

Living Mindfully

Mindfulness is a key practice in working with this law. It enables us to be present in each moment, observing the flow of energy within and around us. Through mindfulness, we can catch and redirect the currents of energy that may be pulling us away from our desired path. By living mindfully, we become attuned to the signs and synchronicities that guide us on our journey. We can recognize when energy is shifting and adapt accordingly, making conscious choices that align with our growth and purpose.

Chapter 7

THE LAW OF CAUSE AND EFFECT

"An effect cannot come before its corresponding cause" – **Aristotle**

> **THE LAW**
>
> The Law of Cause and Effect states that every action generates a corresponding reaction or consequence of equal magnitude and direction. Our thoughts, beliefs, emotions, words, and deeds are causes that set energy in motion, creating ripples that eventually return to us in the form of life situations. Positive actions bring positive results. Negative actions attract negativity back. By becoming conscious of this law, we can uplift our thinking and behavior to create more positive results.

KARMA IN MOTION: MASTERING THE LAW OF CAUSE AND EFFECT

IMAGINE ALWAYS SHOWING UP late for work. You'd likely face consequences like dissatisfied bosses or missed opportunities. This common example demonstrates the universal law that every action creates an effect – known as karma. This principle reveals we shape our realities through thoughts, words, and deeds. Each choice sends ripples, bringing back aligned results.

This profound but often misunderstood law reveals that we shape our reality through our thoughts, words, and deeds. Each choice sends ripples through the universe, bringing back to us corresponding effects. Rather than being victims of circumstances, we are empowered co-creators.

Understanding karma within the Law of Cause and Effect is key. When we plant seeds of positivity through compassionate actions, we grow abundance in our lives. But negative actions yield their own consequences. We reap what we sow on all levels. The good news is each moment offers a chance to redirect our karmic trajectory through conscious choice. We can override old patterns by aligning our behaviors with our highest intentions. For example, if punctuality matters, we act accordingly by preparing early or allowing ample travel time.

By taking responsibility, we learn to harness cause and effect, not be subject to it. Our actions today construct our reality tomorrow. With mindfulness and maturity, we can master this law to author our destinies.

Understanding Karma

Karma is a term that originates from ancient Hindu philosophy and spirituality (Rigveda). It encapsulates the idea that our actions, intentions, and thoughts have consequences not only in this lifetime but also in future ones. While the concept of karma has been associated with reincarnation and the cycle of birth and rebirth, its principles can be applied to our current lives as well.

The Cycle of Cause and Effect

At its core, the Law of Cause and Effect teaches us that our actions are like seeds that we plant in the garden of life. These seeds will eventually sprout and bear fruit, which may be sweet or bitter, depending on the quality of the seeds we have sown. Karma, the timeless law of cause and effect, transcends cultural boundaries and resonates across various belief systems. This intricate web of consequences and actions extends its influence over human existence, shaping destinies and impacting the course of lives. To truly grasp the depth of karma, we must dissect it into its three distinct dimensions: Sanchita Karma, Prarabdha Karma, and Agami Karma. As we embark on this journey of understanding, we'll explore the significance of these karmic facets and their implications for our past, present and future.

> "The law of cause and effect is the silent architect of destiny; every deed echoes in the corridors of time, shaping the path we walk." – **John H Boyd**

SANCHITA KARMA: THE KARMIC BACKLOG

The first dimension of karma, Sanchita Karma, is a profound reservoir of accumulated actions from past lifetimes that are both virtuous and detrimental. It represents the karmic backlog of one's soul, a repository of every deed, intention, and consequence that has yet to be experienced. Think of it as the sum total of your karmic history, an archive of countless lifetimes etched into the fabric of your being.

Imagine Sanchita Karma as a vast library where each book contains the story of a past life tale of love, forgiveness, lessons learned, and lessons yet to unfold. Within this cosmic library, both uplifting and challenging experiences lie in wait, ready to manifest in the tapestry of your existence.

PRARABDHA KARMA: THE UNFOLDING TAPESTRY

As you journey through life, the second dimension of karma, Prarabdha Karma, comes into play. It represents the subset of Sanchita Karma that has ripened and is currently shaping your life's experiences. These are the causes and effects that are unfolding in your present existence, the threads of destiny that you are actively weaving.

Imagine Prarabdha Karma as the loom upon which the threads of your past actions are woven into the fabric of your current reality. The situations, relationships, and events you encounter in this lifetime are the direct results of these past actions. It's as if you are reading a book, one chapter, one page at a time, unaware of the subsequent chapters yet to come.

AGAMI KARMA: THE FORGING OF TOMORROW

The third dimension of karma, Agami Karma, is both dynamic and empowering. It encompasses the karma you are presently creating through your actions, thoughts, and intentions. Agami Karma is the forge of your future experiences, the canvas upon which you paint the masterpiece of your destiny.

Imagine Agami Karma as a blank canvas awaiting the brushstrokes of your intentions and deeds. Each choice you make, everyone thought you harbour, and all the actions you undertake contribute to this ever-evolving masterpiece. While Prarabdha Karma unfolds the chapters of your current life, Agami Karma holds the quill with which you write the chapters of your future.

THE POWER OF AWARENESS AND CHOICE

Understanding the three dimensions of karma empowers you to recognize the profound interplay between past, present, and future. It reinforces the idea that your actions, whether from previous lifetimes or in this moment, hold the power to shape your destiny. With this awareness, you become the architect of your own fate, guided by the principles of cause and effect.

Karma teaches us that our every action, no matter how small, sends out ripples that can grow to create profound effects. Just as drops of water create expanding rings across the surface of a still pond, our words, deeds, and even thoughts make waves that shape our world.

Rather than dwell on or judge the past, the Law of Karma invites us to consciously shape the future. We have the power to rewrite our destinies in each moment by making choices aligned with our highest good. Every day is a new beginning, ripe with potential for us to plant seeds of joy or sorrow, abundance or lack.

We can uplift ourselves and others through simple acts of compassion - a smile that brightens someone's day, a word of encouragement to a struggling friend, or stopping to help a stranger in need. When we lift each other up through deeds big and small, we rise too. With care, courage and wisdom guiding our thoughts, we can steadily redirect our life's path toward light.

Karma and the ripples we make are not burdens but opportunities. The more rays of hope, love and kindness we endeavor to shine into the world, the more beauty and joy we encourage to unfold all around us. By understanding this eternal give and take, we become empowered co-authors of our destinies.

THE KEY POINTS ARE:

- Small positive actions can grow.
- We shape the future through current choices.
- Compassion for others uplifts us.
- Every moment allows us to redirect our course by doing good.

Chapter 8

THE LAW OF COMPENSATION

"The Law of Compensation is constantly working to give us exactly what we earn." **-Brian Tracy**

> ### THE LAW
>
> **The Law of Compensation** affirms that we attract what we radiate. What **you give, you shall receive** - whether positivity, negativity, love or indifference. This universal law maintains equilibrium through equal energy exchange. Our thoughts, words and actions set forces in motion that boomerang back to us, multiplied in kind. Generosity yields abundance. Compassion attracts companionship. Harmful deeds manifest hurt. As we nourish others, we are nourished.

SOWING AND REAPING

THE LAW OF COMPENSATION, a cornerstone of universal principles, asserts that we receive in life what we give. Often described as the law of **"sowing and reaping,"** it embodies the idea that our actions, thoughts, and intentions have consequences that come back to us in kind. To understand this law is to recognize the fundamental principle of cause and effect in our lives.

The Principle of Cause and Effect

At its core, the Law of Compensation is a reflection of the principle of cause and effect. Every action we take, every thought we think, and every intention we hold sets in motion a chain of events that eventually returns to us. This law teaches us that we are not passive observers of our lives but active participants, constantly shaping our reality through our choices and actions.

Much like a farmer who sows seeds in the soil, we sow the seeds of our future experiences through our present actions and intentions. Just as the farmer can expect a harvest in due time, we can anticipate the consequences—positive or negative—of our choices.

> "If you want joy, give joy. If love is what you seek, offer love. If you crave material affluence, help others become prosperous." - **Deepak Chopra**

The Role of Intention

Intention plays a vital role in the Law of Compensation. When our actions are aligned with clear and positive intentions, we increase the likelihood of receiving positive outcomes. Intentions act as the guiding force behind our actions, influencing the quality of what we sow.

It's important to note that intentions go beyond surface-level desires. They reflect our deeper values, beliefs, and aspirations. When we set intentions that are in harmony with our true selves and the greater good, we sow seeds that are more likely to yield abundance and fulfilment.

Patience and Timing

One of the challenges of understanding the Law of Compensation is recognizing that the process may not yield immediate results. Just as a planted seed takes time to sprout and grow, the consequences of our actions may unfold gradually.

Patience and trust in the process are essential. It's easy to become discouraged if we don't see immediate rewards for our efforts. However, the universe operates on its own timeline, and the fruits of our labor may manifest in ways we cannot predict.

Responsibility and Accountability

Embracing the Law of Compensation requires us to take responsibility for our lives. We must acknowledge that we are the architects of our destiny, and our choices have consequences. This recognition empowers us to make conscious decisions and take ownership of our actions. Accountability is not about self-blame but about self-awareness. When we are accountable for our choices, we can learn from our mistakes and make more informed decisions in the future. It is a path to personal growth and empowerment.

The Reciprocal Cycle

The relationship between abundance, gratitude, and the Law of Compensation creates a reciprocal cycle. When we give with a grateful heart, we sow seeds of abundance. As these seeds grow and yield results, we have even more reason to express gratitude, continuing the cycle. This cycle reinforces the idea that giving and receiving are intertwined. When we give generously—whether it's our time, energy, or resources—we open ourselves to receiving in return. This does not mean giving with the expectation of receiving but giving from a place of genuine generosity and goodwill.

Shifting to an Abundance Mindset

Transitioning from a scarcity mindset to an abundance mindset is a transformative journey. Challenge limiting beliefs about deservingness and prosperity. Recognize that the universe is abundant, and there is enough for everyone. When you encounter thoughts of scarcity, replace them with affirmations of abundance. For instance, replace **"I never have enough"** with **"I am a magnet for abundance, and prosperity flows effortlessly into my life."** This shift in mindset will harmonize your actions with the Law of Compensation.

Engaging in the Law of Giving

The Law of Compensation thrives on the principle of giving and receiving. Engage in acts of giving, whether it's your time, resources, or kindness. Be open to opportunities for generosity without expecting anything in return. Observe how these acts of giving create a ripple effect in your life. Consider how unexpected blessings, opportunities, and compensation flow back to you when you give freely and without attachment to outcomes.

Cultivating Gratitude to Complete the Cycle

To fully engage with the reciprocal cycle of giving and receiving, it is vital to cultivate gratitude for what you have already been given. Gratitude energizes the Law of Compensation, motivating us to give freely out of appreciation for our own blessings. It also allows us to recognize the gifts and rewards that flow back to us, even if they come in unexpected ways. Make gratitude a daily practice. Thank the universe in advance for the abundance you desire. When rewards for your actions arrive, no matter how small, acknowledge them with sincere appreciation. Gratitude reminds us that we have already received gifts on this journey, breaking the illusion of scarcity. It completes the cycle of sowing and reaping, allowing this divine law to flow unencumbered through your life.

Chapter 9

THE LAW OF RELATIVITY

"We don't see things as they are, we see them as we are." - **Anaïs Nin**

THE LAW

The Law of Relativity states that nothing has meaning except for the meaning we give it. Experiences in and of themselves are neutral - it is our perspective and judgments that assign them positive or negative meanings. An event that seems like a setback to one person could be seen as an opportunity for growth by another. Challenges become obstacles when we label them as such. Your perspective can be your power or your prison. We can reframe any limitation into a blessing when we change our point of view.

THE POWER OF PERSPECTIVE

This law is based on the principle that nothing has inherent meaning - rather, meaning and significance arise subjectively based on our perspective. An event or circumstance is neutral in and of itself;

the meaning we assign comes from our personal viewpoint and interpretation. By recognizing the subjectivity of meaning, we can empower ourselves to reframe challenges, setbacks, and difficulties by shifting our perspective to see the hidden gifts and opportunities for growth. With an open, flexible mindset, we can transform obstacles into stepping stones and view the events in our lives through a lens of learning, strength, and positivity. The Law of Relativity allows us to take the reins over our experience by choosing an expansive perspective that supports our higher purpose and continual evolution.

Shifting Perspectives

The Law of Relativity teaches us that every challenge we face is relative to our perception. It encourages us to shift our perspective to transform obstacles into opportunities for growth. When confronted with difficulties, it's essential to view them in the context of your own strengths and capabilities.

By changing your viewpoint, you can reframe challenges as stepping stones on your path to manifestation. Instead of perceiving them as insurmountable roadblocks, you see them as valuable lessons and catalysts for personal growth.

> "We can complain because rose bushes have thorns, or rejoice because thorns have roses." - **Alphonse Karr**

Perspective and Perception

At its core, the Law of Relativity teaches us that nothing in the universe is absolute; everything is relative. This means that the nature and quality of any experience or circumstance depend on our perspective and how we choose to perceive it. Two people can face the same situation, yet their experiences and interpretations of it can vary dramatically based on their individual viewpoints.

Compassion and Empathy

Understanding the relativity of experience can also foster compassion and empathy. When we recognize that someone else's pain or joy is relative to their perspective and life circumstances, we are more likely to extend understanding and support.

Empathy arises from the ability to imagine and appreciate another person's perspective, even if it differs from our own. It reminds us that, while we may not fully understand someone else's experience, we can offer kindness and compassion in their journey.

The Power of Perspective

Your perspective is the lens through which you view the world. It is shaped by your beliefs, values, past experiences, and the filters through which you process information. Understanding the power of perspective allows you to recognize that you have the ability to change how you perceive and respond to any situation.

Consider this simple example: Imagine you're caught in a sudden rainstorm without an umbrella. One person might perceive this as an inconvenience and become frustrated, while another might see it as a refreshing and invigorating experience. The rain itself hasn't changed; it's the perspective that determines how it is experienced.

The Gift of Perspective

One of the gifts of the Law of Relativity is the ability to shift our perspective on challenges. Instead of seeing them as obstacles, we can view them as stepping stones on our path to personal development and fulfilment.

For instance, a career setback may initially appear as a failure. However, from a broader perspective, it may be a redirection toward a more fulfilling and meaningful path. By reframing challenges in this way, we can maintain a positive outlook and continue our journey with resilience.

Shifting Your Perspective

Shifting your perspective is a conscious choice that empowers you to **see the silver lining in challenging situations.** It allows you to reframe difficulties as opportunities for growth and transformation. Here are some strategies to help you shift your perspective:

- **Seek Different Viewpoints:** Engage in conversations with others who have different perspectives and experiences. This can broaden your understanding and help you see situations from various angles.

- **Challenge Negative Thoughts:** When negative or limiting thoughts arise, challenge them by asking yourself if they are based on facts or assumptions. Often, negative thoughts are based on unfounded beliefs that can be reframed.

- **Embrace Change:** Recognize that change is a natural part of life. Instead of resisting it, embrace it as an opportunity for growth and new experiences.

- **Practice Mindfulness:** Mindfulness meditation can help you become more aware of your thoughts and emotions in the present moment. By observing them without judgment, you can choose how to respond and shift your perspective.

Finding Meaning in Challenges

Life is filled with challenges, and the Law of Relativity reminds us that the significance of these challenges is relative to our perspective. While some difficulties may seem insurmountable, others can be seen as valuable opportunities for personal growth and learning.

The Role of Challenges in Personal Growth

Challenges, whether they are in the form of setbacks, obstacles, or adversity, often serve as catalysts for personal growth. They push us out of our comfort zones, encourage resilience, and provide opportunities to develop new skills and strengths.

Consider the story of a young tree growing in a forest. When the forest experiences a drought, the tree's roots are forced to grow deeper in search of water. In doing so, the tree becomes more resilient and better equipped to withstand future challenges. Similarly, challenges in our lives can lead to profound personal growth and transformation.

The Power Lies Within Us

Each of us has the power to shift the way we experience the world by altering our perspective. Difficult situations often arise to facilitate growth, even when the reason or lesson is not yet visible. Rather than react with frustration, we can pause, breathe deeply, and open our minds to new ways of seeing. With an expansive perspective, we can turn adversities into opportunities. When we change the way we view challenges, their very nature is transformed. As we awaken to our own resilience, wisdom, and strength of spirit, we become empowered to shape all of life's circumstances into catalysts for positive transformation.

Chapter 10

THE LAW OF POLARITY

"Wherever there is light, there is shadow. The key is appreciating them both." -**Tom Althouse**

> ### THE LAW
>
> **The Law of Polarity** reveals the dance between opposites that creates our world. **Where there is light, there must also be shadow.** Where positivity blooms, negativity waits to be transformed. This principle of duality is the heartbeat pulsing through all of life. **Darkness and light play together** in an eternal interweaving. Like yin and yang, contrasting elements interact to form the vivid mosaic of existence. Now, you may see opposites as contradiction - **but in truth, they are two halves of one whole.** Darkness is just unlit light. Cold is the absence of heat. Evil is a call for more love. Without one, the other could not exist.

THE FUNDAMENTAL DANCE OF DUALITIES

THE LAW OF POLARITY stands as one of the most profound universal laws, revealing that all of existence is composed of dualities. Like two sides of the same coin, opposites are deeply interconnected. Light needs darkness just as day relies on night. This law conveys that contrasting poles exist everywhere - in nature, in society, and within our own psyches.

By embracing the full spectrum between extremes, we can find balance, integration and wisdom. The Law of Polarity beckons us to dance gracefully with life's contradictions and harness the creative potential birthed from the tensions between opposites.

Learning from Contrasts

The dance between opposites can help us grow. By bravely exploring the light and dark parts of ourselves, we discover we are complex beings. The highs and lows we face teach us important lessons. Loss removes excess and makes room for new blessings. Hard times build strength, wisdom and compassion. Challenges test our commitment, like pressure turning carbon into diamonds. Yet, for hardship to bear fruit, we must face it with care, not run away in fear. See each contrast as a teacher for your growth. By blending life's many shades into a full understanding, you'll find the light you sought outside now shines from within you and through all.

The Light and Dark Within

The interplay between light and darkness perhaps best encapsulates polarity. The beauty of a sunrise is defined by the preceding stillness of night. In the same vein, our most luminous joys are sharpened against sorrows. Within each of us, light and shadow coexist. Our potential manifests most powerfully when we nourish all aspects of ourselves with compassion.

The cycles between day and night reflect nature's intrinsic rhythms. As we align ourselves with these natural oscillations between activity and rest, we discover resilience. Daily practices of self-care can anchor us during active days, while the playful enjoyment of night energizes us for dawn's light.

Beyond day and night, the Law of Polarity weaves together all of existence. **Winter's bareness gives rise to spring's blossoms.** Hardship strengthens our spirits like metal forged through fire. Problems resolved deepen wisdom. Muscles broken down through exertion grow back stronger.

By recognizing the natural balanced dance between extremes, we can graciously accept both the highs and lows of our journey. Each experience gifts us opportunities for learning, even if the lessons are initially veiled.

THE INTERPLAY OF LOVE AND FEAR

In the realm of emotions, love and fear represent a profound duality. Love arises from connection. It breeds compassion, joy, generosity, and unity. Fear often springs from disconnection. It engenders polarization, anxiety, and isolation.

We all feel pulled between these opposing forces within relationships, communities, and the world at large. Global events that seed fear and separation activate love when people unite through hope and kindness. The Law of Polarity empowers us to counter fear with the light of love.

On an individual level, we can balance fear with daily practices that cultivate connection, whether through mindfulness, time in nature, or personal growth. By finding equilibrium between hope and despair, trust and caution, acceptance and discernment, we navigate life's emotional oscillation with stability.

THE ROLE OF PERSPECTIVE

Perception serves as the compass guiding our experience of polarity. How we perceive challenges and blessings shapes our emotional responses. Painful experiences provide opportunities to reframe our perspective and unearth purpose in adversity.

Consider seeing problems as teachers rather than obstacles. Each one bears a lesson if we open our minds to learning. Mistakes morph from failures to stepping stones when viewed as feedback for improvement. Similarly, an unexpected change in plans redirects us towards new horizons.

With an outlook of curiosity instead of judgment, we recognize that what first appears positive or negative is truly dependent on our unique vantage point. By consciously reframing our perspective, we can uncover the hidden gifts contained within both peaks and valleys.

The Art of Living in Balance

The Law of Polarity reminds us that too much of any one thing inevitably activates its opposite. When we move towards extremes, universal forces bring us back towards equilibrium.

Consider exercise and rest. Too much exertion overworks the body, manifesting as fatigue or burnout. This prompts a natural desire to replenish through relaxation and recovery. Conversely, excessive rest leads to a lack of strength and energy, motivating us to get active. Through balanced oscillation between activity and rest, our health and vitality flourish.

This interplay of opposites maintains equilibrium on emotional and mental levels too. If we repress anger, it intensifies until we acknowledge and then release it. Obsessive attachment to desires often backfires, with the very fixation repelling what we seek. By modulating between spectrums, we manifest goals with grace.

Flowing with Natural Rhythms

At its core, the Law of Polarity is a potent reminder to flow with life's natural rhythms. Like seasons, cycles perpetually come and go. Resisting their circulation breeds stress. As we attune ourselves to these rhythms, we begin to perceive their hidden order.

Inactivity: seek periods of quiet contemplation to soak in insights. Between phases of work, nurture in leisure and play. When faced with loss, make space for grieving before opening up to joy. Times of hardship are followed by ease. Ebb and flow through polarities in step with divine timing.

When we entrain our minds and bodies to nature's cadence, growth unfolds organically. Just as plants unfurl their petals only when conditions are optimal, desired outcomes manifest effortlessly once we're aligned with natural rhythms. By riding the waves between dualities, we surf the creative forces of the cosmos.

Integrating Duality into Wholeness

Recognize that within every loss, there is an opportunity for renewal. In times of fear, courage is strengthened. Criticism, when accepted with equanimity, fuels improvement. By extracting lessons from both pleasant and unpleasant experiences, our worldview grows more holistic. Soon, we realize that light and dark are our sacred partners, equipping us for life.

Chapter 11

THE LAW OF RHYTHM

"Accept that all of life is in motion. We live in an ocean of constant waves of change. When we choose not to struggle against it, we are able to find our flow." **-Christopher McCandless**

The Law

The Law of Rhythm states that life unfolds in **cycles, seasons, and waves**—from birth to death, light to dark, activity to rest. Each phase has value and purpose. Winter fertilizes spring. Night restores day. Difficulties strengthen us. Without the full spectrum of experiences, we cannot appreciate the highs as much. By accepting the natural oscillations of life, we stop resisting what is. When we embrace each stage, seeing challenges as opportunities, we gain the fluidity to manifest our desires. Cycles naturally transition. Trust in their wisdom. Each low holds the seeds of a new high. Rhythm brings balance and rebirth.

Riding the Waves of Life's Rhythms

Have you noticed how life seems to move in cycles? **How do some seasons feel full of energy and growth while others are more solemn and still?** How do circumstances often appear to swing between lack and abundance, chaos and calm? These ups and downs are no coincidence. They reflect the natural ebb and flow of the universe, pulsing to the beat of its own rhythm. Recognizing and understanding this profound Law of Rhythm can help you navigate life's twists and turns with more ease, purpose and inner peace.

The Cycles Around Us

For instance, when you suddenly lose a job, relationship or a loved one, the sense of loss can be devastating. Understandably, you may resist and resent that change uprooted your stability. Yet with time and self-care, a new vision emerges. This ending made space for unexpected gifts like exploring new careers, meeting a more compatible partner, or cherishing memories of one passed. The phase of loss, while painful, contained opportunity.

The Wisdom in Each Cycle

Each phase of life's cycles carries a unique gift, if we open our eyes to receive it. In times of energetic expansion, seeds of intention blossom and manifest. Periods of retreat nourish roots for future growth. Within loss, space clears for new blessings. Hardship cultivates resilience, creativity, and connection. Difficulties passed initiate fresh starts. Cycles teach impermanence; all conditions eventually shift. Attune yourself to each season's particular medicine. Harvest insights from every experience. Then when cycles turn like pages in a book, you read each new chapter with understanding.

The River Within You

Releasing rigid attachment and trusting in the flow, while profoundly peaceful once cultivated, can feel extremely challenging at first. Our minds cling to illusions of control. But gracefully surrendering to changes and cycles requires compassion for ourselves and repeated practice. Much like building muscle, we grow our capacity to 'go with the flow' gradually through small daily actions. Over time, harmonizing with life's currents can start to feel more natural.

The challenge becomes an opportunity. Change morphs into growth. Suddenly, you're surfing life's waves rather than feeling drowned by them.

Cultivating Your Inner Oasis

Yet even on the smoothest river, some turbulence is inevitable. That's why nurturing inner balance is so crucial. Your inner equilibrium acts like the sturdy mast of a sailboat, keeping you upright when rocked by waves.

Take time regularly to check in with yourself. How are you faring physically, mentally, emotionally, and spiritually? Make any needed adjustments to restore alignment and prevent burnout during especially high-intensity cycles.

Quiet contemplation and mindfulness practices help center you in stillness beneath the surface currents. Gratitude lifts your gaze to appreciate beauty amidst the ride's commotion.

By cultivating this inner oasis of peace using whatever practices resonate most, you generate a wellspring of tranquillity. Life's rhythms can't disturb your core when it's deeply rooted.

Riding the Cycles

Tune into your own energy levels each day or week. **When do you naturally peak or ebb?** You can start harnessing these cycles by matching activities to your rhythm - schedule creative work or social activities during energetic upswings and restorative practices when energy retreats. Rituals like meditating at sunrise, exercising midday, or journaling before bed can sync your days with natural cycles for optimal flow. Anticipate periods when anxieties may surge, preparing tools to return your mind to balance.

Get to know the river within you, and you can harness its power.

Let's recap principles to remember as you flow with life's rhythms:

- The only constant is change. Flow with the seasons; don't fight the tides.

- Tune into natural cycles around and within you. This builds self-knowledge.

- Anticipate ups and downs. Prepare practices to maintain balance through each.

- Release attachment to rigid outcomes. Trust in the flow.

- Mindfully choose actions to align with each phase. Discern when to ride a wave or redirect it.

- Cultivate inner tranquillity beyond the surface currents. Your purpose is the anchor.

By understanding these natural rhythms, we learn not only to float through stormy seasons but to actively harness their potential. With each crest, we are lifted a little higher in understanding our journey.

Chapter 12

THE LAW OF GENDER

"The entire universe is made up of the constant interaction between Yin and Yang." **- Helen Keller**

THE LAW

The Law of Gender states that **all life contains both masculine and feminine energies, yin and yang**. The dance between these complementary qualities drives creation. Masculine energy is assertive, focused, and directed. Feminine energy is receptive, collective, and nurturing. Neither is superior; both are vital. Ideally, in balance, excess of one causes distortion. As social beings, we may assume rigid gender roles. However, we each contain male and female essences regardless of biological sex. Integrating our wholeness allows full expression of power. Through harmonizing gender energies within, we progress spiritually. Partnership thrives when both are honored equally.

Honoring the Masculine and Feminine

True empowerment arises when we harmonize the masculine and feminine within us all. Neither essence is better, only different in nature. The assertive drives of the masculine must be balanced by the receptive qualities of the feminine. As we calm resistance to embracing our wholeness, we gain newfound strength. Meet your inner polarities with courage and care. By loving each other equally, their synergy manifests our highest potential. Like the wings of a bird, both halves soar together.

The Dance of Dualities

Life is a dynamic dance of dualities. Dark and light, strength and vulnerability, chaos and order - these are but some of the complementary energies that make up the cosmic choreography we move to. An essential rhythm in this dance is the interplay between our inner masculine and feminine aspects. By understanding and integrating these, we can discover a profound universal truth: harmony is born not by negating any energy but by embracing the full spectrum of who we are.

What are these masculine and feminine energies? Imagine them not as fixed gender traits but as fluid qualities we all share in varying degrees. The masculine draws on focused, analytical, and assertive attributes. It provides direction through clarity of thought and strength of will. The feminine encompasses intuition, cooperation, creativity, and compassion. It is the receptive, nurturing flow that complements and balances the driven masculine energy. We each have access to both, yet often develop an imbalance by suppressing one.

In ancient wisdom, myths and symbols across cultures reflected this dance of dualities. The Chinese concept of yin and yang illuminates how seeming opposites contain each other and form a greater whole. God and Goddess archetypes remind us that creation arises from partnership, not domination. Modern science echoes this truth - it takes both assertion and reception to manifest anything.

THE 12 UNIVERSAL LAWS

By looking within, we can observe our inner dance in motion. Do your masculine qualities like logic and decisiveness dominate, while your softer side goes unexpressed? Or does your open-hearted nature thrive while your directionality falters? There is no ideal balance, only awareness.

HERE ARE SOME WAYS TO EXPLORE YOUR INNER RHYTHMS:

- Notice when you cling to one mode and avoid its counterpart. Meet whatever arises with acceptance rather than resistance.

- Play with expressing dormant energies. If you are highly analytical, make time for creative activities. If you are highly intuitive, practice logic-building.

- Examine your most fulfilling relationships. Do they involve an equitable exchange of complementary energies that allows both to flourish?

- Use visualizations to picture masculine and feminine energies dancing together, flowing into each other, creating harmony.

There is no set formula - only your unique rhythm. As you learn to move with your inner music, you build the courage and compassion to embrace all of who you are. By integrating our dualities, we find balance, power and the freedom to manifest our highest potential. We come to see that the dance of life takes place not despite our differences but because of them.

So, as you walk your path, remember you have all the steps you need if you allow your inner energies to cooperate, not compete. May the dance fill you with grace.

Chapter 13

LETTING GO

The Myth of the Perfect Time

Stop Waiting for the Right Time

WE ALL HARBOR DREAMS, just waiting for the "right" moment to pursue them. Maybe you've been eager to apply for the job but want to polish your resume first. Or perhaps you've envisioned starting your own business but don't feel ready until you've got every detail worked out. The law of inspired action also debunks the myth of the "perfect" time. This law states that we must act on sparks of inspiration when they strike rather than waiting for ideal conditions.

It's tempting to hold off on manifesting goals until conditions seem perfect—enough savings, the ideal qualifications, or clarity on every unknown. But banking on some fabled right time sets you up for perpetual waiting. Life brings unpredictable chaos no matter how polished our plans are. Detours often unlock the very resources we need to succeed. By taking action before you feel completely ready, you give yourself the chance to course-correct toward the end goal. Waiting for the mythic "perfect" moment means your ambitions may never materialize.

The Law of Inspired Action also debunks the myth of the "perfect" time. This law states that we must act on sparks of inspiration when they strike rather than waiting for ideal conditions. As the text notes, "Passion is rare—don't waste it wondering whether conditions are perfect." If we hold off on chasing inspiration until everything aligns flawlessly, we may miss out entirely. Or that the initial fire driving us toward a dream may fade. By taking imperfect action when our enthusiasm swells, we build the energy and insight to carry us through obstacles bound to arise later. What looks easy from the outside takes persistently showing up through difficulty. Had masters waited for some fabled "right" time to begin developing their talents, they may have never achieved excellence in their craft. Progress lies not in waiting endlessly but in moving boldly towards the pull of inspiration.

Imperfect Action Beats Perfect Planning

We often presume competence must come before commitment. But the truth is, action builds skill. What looks smooth from the outside actually takes repeated, imperfect tries behind the scenes. Even masters had to start somewhere through trial and error.

Rather than over-preparing, understand that some stumbling is part of any learning process. Diving in before you feel completely ready gives you the chance to self-correct based on real experience. It allows you to iterate as you gather feedback and discern what works.

So don't get paralyzed by the illusion of others' seamless journeys. Know that behind the scenes lie countless clumsy starts and mistakes. Give yourself permission to be a student when undertaking any new endeavor. Progress comes through repetitively showing up.

By taking imperfect action rather than waiting until everything looks perfect, you set the stage for growth. You build real-world intuition vital for excelling in any domain. Don't overthink preparation - dive in and trust that often the best way forward is by simply starting.

Tune Into Emerging Patterns

Rather than seeing conditions as "good" or "bad", recognize all situations contain seeds of opportunity. Chaos carries the raw materials for your goals amidst the disorder—if you're willing to work with what you have.

Trying to control all details sets you up for frustration. But responding to circumstances as they unfold builds strength. Each challenge carries lessons to apply next time. By taking imperfect action, you can start discerning forward momentum even amidst setbacks.

Here are three ways to spur progress:

- **Notice what's working** – Instead of beating yourself up over mistakes, focus on what is working and do more of that.

- **Adjust your aim** – If some targets now seem unrealistic given new contexts, pick more pertinent goals.

- **Give each attempt attentiveness** – Don't multitask or skip review, even when things don't go as hoped. Full focus unlocks key insights for wise next steps.

Pivot Toward Where Energy Flows

Fear of failure often fuels waiting—we withhold action until we know just how to avoid mistakes. But missteps are integral to mastery on any endeavor. By taking successive imperfect actions, you start discerning a forward pull toward your true aims. Some efforts may nudge you to recalibrate your goals.

Rather than waiting for assurance, you have the "right dream", chase every spark of inspiration before it extinguishes. Passion is rare—don't waste it wondering whether conditions are perfect. By moving toward what calls you, answers arise in time. Ask yourself:

What ignites my enthusiasm and dissolves distraction even when things get hard? Your internal compass knows the way even if you cannot yet see it. By acting on inspiration before certainty, you build the energy needed for the next wise step to emerge.

Progress Comes From Doing, Not Waiting

We might wait years for the perfect conditions to pursue treasured goals. But the "right" moment is a myth—there will always be uncertainty about applying for a dream job or launching that innovative business. By taking action before you feel ready, skill builds. Momentum snowballs opportunity even amidst imperfection.

Imagine each day holds just one missing jigsaw piece to manifest your goal. By actively working the puzzle with whatever pieces exist already, more come your way. But leave the board idle too long, awaiting "perfect" conditions, and you'll never experience the satisfaction of a completed vision.

Our gravestones list two dates with a dash in between representing our lifespan. Yet that dash is where all of life's purpose and meaning resides. We are not defined by the day we were born or the day we die but by the quality of the journey in between. Life is meant for pursuing dreams, connecting to others, and learning through experience. Don't let your dash remain empty, waiting for some mythic "right" time. Fill it by taking imperfect action, immersing yourself fully, and engaging each moment. True fulfilment comes not from waiting endlessly but from moving steadily forward with passion right now. The perfect time is whenever you choose to start.

Progress depends not on waiting for assurance but on moving steadily with what you have right now. By acting before you feel fully prepared, you build the maturity and knowledge needed to manifest your biggest dreams.

You Have to Clear in Order to Create

Clear Your Clutter, Manifest Your Dreams

When was the last time you truly took stock of the sheer volume of stuff crowding your home? If you're like most people living in the modern world, the answer is probably "too long ago to recall". Your home likely contains piles of unused possessions stuffed in closets, drawers overflowing with clothing not worn in years, and countless knick-knacks gathering dust on shelves. This clutter might seem harmless, but it takes up both physical and mental space that could be put to much better use, attracting exciting new manifestations into your life.

The Negative Effects of Clutter

Increased stress and anxiety. Clutter around the home creates visual chaos that can overstimulate the brain. This triggers the release of the stress hormone cortisol. Chronic clutter has been linked to increased anxiety, depression, and fatigue.

Cognitive overwhelm. Clutter competes for our attention and makes it harder to focus. A cluttered home requires using more mental energy just to process visual information, leaving less capacity for higher-level thinking and completing tasks.

Wasted time. A cluttered home requires more time for basic tasks like getting ready in the morning, finding items, cleaning, etc. When spaces are disorganized, routine tasks just take more time and energy.

Unhealthy behaviors. Cluttered spaces promote more impulsive behaviors like emotional shopping, overspending, and hoarding in some individuals. The visual chaos interferes with decision-making abilities.

Sleep interference. Visual disorders in a bedroom have been scientifically shown to disrupt sleep quality and duration. This contributes to increased tiredness and irritability.

Interpersonal tension. A home filled with clutter can promote conflict among family members, especially for those with different organizational tolerances and preferences. It also causes embarrassment and prevents inviting others over.

The key takeaway from the research is that clutter drains mental resources, creates emotional discord, disrupts health behaviors, and prevents homes from functioning efficiently. Taming the clutter has wide-ranging quality-of-life benefits.

The Weight of Your Stuff Anchors You Down

All of the things you own carry an energetic weight – and when your space is highly cluttered, that accumulated weight acts like an anchor, holding you back from moving forward. Just as trying to swim while wearing heavy boots would slow your pace to a crawl, having an environment dense with clutter makes it exponentially harder to progress towards goals and welcome positive change. Clearing out your unused belongings lifts this anchor so you can fluidly move towards the amazing manifestations waiting for you.

Trees Shed Their Leaves To Grow again Each Spring

In the cycle of growth in nature, trees are forced to completely shed their leaves before welcoming in new buds. There simply isn't enough space for fresh green growth when last autumn's faded leaves still cling to every branch. Your home environment works the same way – if the old remnants of yesteryear still take up space in your drawers and on your shelves, there is no room for the new growth ready to burst forth when spring comes. It is only by completely clearing away the old that you make space for new inspirations to flow in.

READY FOR A FRESH START? TACKLE YOUR CLUTTER!

If you feel stuck in place, drained of inspiration, or simply ready for a wholesale revitalization of your environment, then the time has come to do a deep cleanse of clutter. Give every room, closet, and drawer the scrutiny it deserves and clear out anything you don't absolutely love or regularly use. Bag up donations, trash what has completely worn out its stay, and find better homes for things that belong elsewhere.

BE RUTHLESS – AND REWARD YOURSELF AFTER!

This process can be emotionally and physically exhausting, so be sure to reward yourself afterwards! Plan a relaxing evening soaking in the bathtub after an afternoon of purging old files from your home office. Schedule a nap or movie night as soon as the last unneeded item goes out the door. You deserve appreciation for doing the tough inner work of letting go.

WRITE DOWN GOALS FOR YOUR NEWLY CLEAR SPACE

As you gaze around newly refreshed spaces brimming with open potential, take time to thoughtfully consider what you'd like to manifest in this blank slate for the future. Jot down goals, dreams, inspirations – let your imagination flow freely! Having this clarity of intention allows the universe to start sending precisely what you ask for.

By routinely clearing clutter and setting intentions for desired outcomes, you enable your environment to become a receptive vessel for positive growth rather than a stagnant pool.

Shedding Familial Limitations

The Weight of Family History

I COME FROM A long line of dreamers—those who aspire for more but fail to achieve it. My ancestors sought fortunes through get-rich schemes rather than honest work. They hoped lady luck would one day smile upon them. But the winning lottery ticket forever eluded their grasp.

Generations of dashed hopes and expectations have weighed upon me since childhood. **"Success is for other people, not us,"** family members would say, echoing the words they had heard decades ago. This fixed mindset infected my thinking like a virus, eroding any sparks of ambition.

Resignation in School

In school, I set no goals, made no plans, and drifted along aimlessly, assuming fate would determine my destiny. If I did well on an exam, I attributed it to chance, not effort. Why try when the deck was stacked against me? My ancestors left me no legacy beyond quiet resignation. In young adulthood, the siren song of hereditary failure beckoned me to obey its commands: **"Don't attempt what you can't achieve."** Its chorus rang in my mind.

The Easy Refuge

Each time I confronted a challenge, the refuge of quitting appeared easier than the risk of trying. But one day, revelations struck me about this hereditary thinking.

> **Our minds—not our DNA—drive our ACTIONS**

Past generations did not biologically transmit attitudes through blood. Their infected thinking spread through learned words and actions passed down to each succeeding generation.

Discovering My Mindset

Once I realized I had the power to change my life, I started taking steps to improve things. I stopped blaming outside forces for my problems and took responsibility for my own negative thinking. If I had low expectations for myself, I worked to change my mindset. Bit by bit, I set new goals for myself until I achieved some success. Eventually, mentors helped guide me to even greater accomplishments.

Today, sometimes, that voice from my past pops up, telling me to give up hope. But now I recognize that voice and know I have a choice. I can either listen to those doubtful thoughts from my past or actively work towards growth and success. My future is up to me - I have the power to break free from old ways of limited thinking. With an open and growth-focused mindset, I am free to reach my potential.

Stages of Metamorphosis

> My metamorphosis towards a transformed mindset has unfolded across four key stages:
> **Awareness** - Initially realizing the self-limiting beliefs I inherited from past generations
> **Accountability** - Accepting responsibility for my own mindset and expectations, not blaming external forces
> **Exploration** - Discovering and testing new goals not bound by family history
> **Ascent** - Committing to higher visions of achievement fueled by an open mindset

The Larva Stage

In the "awareness" stage, I remained in a larval phase of resignation, not fully recognizing my self-imposed constraints. Like a caterpillar munching the same leaves day after day, I operated on autopilot —accepting without questioning my alleged predestined mediocrity.

The first cracks in my chrysalis emerged when I witnessed peers with similar family backgrounds accomplish goals I had dismissed as impossible for me. Their examples revealed that hereditary thinking lived in my mind, not my genes. This realization marked my emergence into the next stage.

The Pupa Phase

In the "accountability" phase, I transitioned into the pupa stage. I examined my thoughts like a moth-in-waiting, scrutinizing its cocoon before undergoing radical change. By analyzing stories, patterns and assumptions handed down through generations, I realized how this thinking restricted me. My personal expectations, not inherited traits, dictated my future.

This truth both stung and liberated me. Stung, because it meant I had actively chosen self-imposed limits. Yet it liberated me too, because this meant that with changed thinking, I could take ownership of mapping a bolder direction. My future was mine to shape.

Testing My Wings

In the "exploration" stage, I began stretching beyond familiar comfort zones, as hesitantly as a new moth testing its wings. With mentors' support, I identified untried academic and career interests that once appeared off-limits. Slowly but surely, I invested in new aspirations like enrolling in night courses — small steps to exercise my freedom to pursue new horizons beyond my ancestry.

Now in the "ascent" phase, I stand tall, looking out at the new horizons I've reached. It took staying dedicated through unsure times, doubting myself sometimes, and even occasionally sliding back. Breaking free of that resigned mindset wasn't fast or simple. But getting out of the limitations I had made for myself unleashed dreams hidden deep within. Even though the journey continues, I enjoy flying freely at last – creating my life's story how I choose.

Now, when I look ahead, I see lots of opportunities instead of limits. My family's history is in the past, but my story is still happening. I'm really thankful for those who helped me and for the inner strength that let me take this trip. Some days, old doubts might come back. But I've built mental muscles to lift myself above those thoughts to higher places. Like an eagle flying free, not held down by where it used to live, I'm also pushed up by new belief in my ability to grow and do more. This is the view from the top - an open sky inviting me to worlds I haven't discovered yet.

Recognizing the Need for Change

"Your time is limited, so don't waste it living someone else's life. Don't be trapped by dogma - which is living with the results of other people's thinking. Don't let the noise of other's opinions drown out your own inner voice. And most important, have the courage to follow your heart and intuition." - **Steve Jobs**

Navigating Your True Path

Life presents many crossroads where one direction leads down a worn path of complacency while another winds up through new territory full of personal growth and meaning. Like sailors on the open seas, we must learn to harness our inner compass to guide us toward fulfilling destinations rather than simply drifting wherever the currents carry us.

What does it mean to listen to your inner wisdom? Consider someone stuck in an unrewarding job, mainly for a stable income. They may have once felt passionate about their work but now dread the daily grind. An inner voice deep down tries telling them something essential is missing in order to feel truly alive and motivated. However, fear and societal pressure keep muting this internal navigation system.

On the other hand, think of someone who courageously made a major life change to pursue what they love, whether opening a small business doing meaningful work or restructuring their lifestyle around core values. At first, it involved risk and uncertainty. But soon, this path cultivated energy and a sense of purpose that had been missing before. By taking a chance guided by inner truths rather than outward validation, they charted a course aligned with their soul's true desires.

We all have this innate inner compass meant to guide us toward our highest potentials and most fulfilling expressions of self. It tries to keep us on course when we start drifting into stagnation or quiet resignation.

Some common signs the Universe wants you to check your positioning:

- Feeling chronically unmotivated, lifeless, or despairing about relationships or work that used to engage you

- Letting fear of failure or societal "shoulds" drive major decisions rather than authentic desires

- Sensing something vital is missing or there's more out there waiting to be explored

- Struggling more than seems reasonable with self-defeating patterns or behaviors

- Feeling trapped in situations draining your energy and suffocating personal growth

- Experiencing unusual restlessness, impatience, or jumpiness on the status quo

- Having vivid dreams prodding you to take risks, embrace change, or stop postponing dreams

- Catching yourself envying friends living more freely or purposefully

- Hearing inner voices saying, "This isn't you anymore" about major parts of life

- Seeing synchronistic signs like repetitious numbers or chance meetings nudging you

- Trouble sleeping or restless, unsatisfying sleep

- Lack of appetite, overeating, drinking alcohol to excess

- Inexplicable anxiousness or sadness

- Difficulty concentrating or mental fogginess

- Withdrawing from social connections and activities

Pay attention when you sport several of these, suggesting an inner realignment is necessary for greater fulfilment. It may be time to do some deep exploration about who you really are and what you truly want next.

If these resonate with you, take heart - it's never too late for a course correction. The key is taking time to reconnect with your inner self by trying activities like:

- Journaling to unpack your core values, childhood dreams, or ideal visions of the future

- Spending meditative time in nature to calm your mind from its worry-patterns

- Having candid conversations with trusted friends about where you're feeling misalignment

As you dedicate effort towards tuning into your inner truths again, you regain clarity about which new bearings to set. It takes courage to change tides, to sow seeds that feel true to your soul, though the outcome remains unseen. But what is life without a little adventure? Let your spirit be the compass, however imperfect, guiding you always back home to yourself.

Let the Universe Handle the How

The Freedom of Letting Go

As you journey toward your dreams and ambitions, you likely have a vision of how you'll get there. Maybe you've plotted out every step along the path to that coveted corner office. Or perhaps you know exactly which courses you must ace to land your dream job. There's comfort in having a plan - it gives us direction and hope. But clinging too tightly to a fixed agenda can also lock us into rigid thinking, blocking unseen possibilities. By releasing attachment to the "how", we create space for the unexpected to find us.

Relinquishing Control

Navigating life can involve relinquishing control at times, which can be like learning a new language. I've been so accustomed to planning every detail, especially during holidays, that any deviation feels like a misstep. I vividly remember an incident when my best friend got her car stuck. We were at her brother's house, and their calm response to her car getting stuck contrasted sharply with my panicked internal reaction. Her sister-in-law's nonchalance taught me a valuable lesson: sometimes, things just require a cool head and a readiness to adapt. I'm striving to emulate that attitude. It's a gradual process of unlearning the need to micromanage every aspect. The realization hit hard that striving for control amidst unpredictability only leads to exhaustion. I've started paying attention to the signs around me, like a sailor gauging the winds, adjusting my course while keeping sight of the ultimate destination. This journey toward letting go of control isn't easy, but I'm finding that by remaining open-minded and flexible, unexpected opportunities present themselves. The road to success isn't a linear one, and embracing the twists and turns might just lead to remarkable discoveries.

Stay Open to Surprises

So rather than micromanaging every "how", focus on clarifying the "what" – the purpose behind your dream. Knowing what truly matters anchors you, while keeping options open as to how to get there. Like a sailor who knows their destination but understands wind and weather may reroute the voyage, purpose fuels flexibility.

Tune Into Your Changing Environment

Life brings disruption even in the best-laid plans. The pandemic taught us just how rapidly entire systems can be thrown into upheaval. But fluctuation is inevitable, with or without external shocks. Priorities shift, new opportunities arise, and circumstances transform relationships or resources in a heartbeat. The only constant is change itself.

Trying to control everything amidst unpredictability will leave you depleted. But regularly checking in with your environment helps you recognize vital signals. Just as sailors continually scan conditions to adjust course, assess whether parts of your plan need updating. Be ready to incorporate unexpected blessings that nudge you naturally closer to your goal.

Maybe a chance encounter sparks an idea more aligned with emerging priorities. Or changing financial situations shift how much you can reasonably take on. By staying attuned as contexts morph, you'll organically tweak how you manifest dreams without compromising the vision.

> **HERE'S MY ADVICE:**
>
> - Focus on major milestones, not every little step. Define the key wins that show you're headed in the right direction. Planning every detail just cramps your style.
>
> - Set reminders to check where you're at, this gives you a chance to incorporate new avenues you have discovered.
>
> - Keep an open mind. What seems impossible now might become possible with a lucky break. But you'll only act on those game-changing chances if you're paying attention. So pay attention.

The road to success is rarely a straight line. To really go places, you need the freedom to zigzag. So, toss the rigid rulebook. Get curious about fresh routes. And remember - the journeys that transform us most often start with an unexpected first step.

Be Ready to Pivot

When chasing big goals, you have to stay nimble. Don't get so stuck on your original plan that you miss unexpected shortcuts. Sure, map out the general route - but leave room for detours. By staying loose, you can jump on opportunities you'd otherwise miss.

Trust the Currents

Some of the greatest barriers to goals lie not in external logistics but in our over-management of how we envision the path unfolding. Attachments to previous plans blind us as circumstances change shape around us. But by loosening the grip on rigidity, we permit external currents to carry us.

Imagine your goal as a ship sailing across the sea. Your purpose is the anchor, maintaining direction by knowing where you wish to arrive amidst uncertainty. By tuning into signals from the environment, you can fluidly shift course to ride the most favorable winds toward your destination. Trust that releasing the "how" magnifies your readiness to capitalize on arising blessings nudging you where you wish to go. Allowing flexibility fuels, rather than compromises, the journey.

So stay anchored in your purpose and direction, but let go of fixations on precise steps. As you monitor horizons for opportunities awakened by shifting landscapes, you remain ready to catch the optimal currents to efficiently arrive exactly where you wish to be. By simply permitting rather than controlling, you unlock the power of synchronicity already built into the world around you.

Cultivating Inner Peace Amidst Uncertainty

Releasing rigid attachment to plans provides the openness to capitalize on arising blessings. But relinquishing that sense of control can also initially feel unsettling. The mind craves certainty. By cultivating inner peace, we find calm within uncertainty. When you notice anxiety arise as plans veer off-course, pause. Breathe deeply and reconnect to the present moment. Remind yourself that detours may lead to unimagined destinations even more fulfilling than the original goal. See each unexpected twist as an opportunity to practice flexibility and trust. Let go of needing to know precisely how events will unfold. Peace amidst uncertainty emerges when we allow life's currents to guide rather than attempt to grasp tightly. Progress manifests effortlessly when we flow in faith. Inner tranquillity amidst outer fluidity lets intuition determine when to stay the course versus when to change tack. By relaxing into each moment just as it is, we begin to trust the perfection of how our path is unfolding.

The Open Hand Philosophy

Seeking Goals with an Open Hand

You likely have goals you feel compelled to achieve—a promotion, buying a house, starting a business. The normal mindset is to grip these goals tightly with wrapped fingers, worried they'll slip away if you're not careful. But this only creates stress. There is a better approach.

The open hand philosophy advocates desiring goals while simultaneously accepting not getting them. This concept goes hand-in-hand with the previous chapter's message of releasing attachment to outcomes by trusting in yourself instead of needing certain results for happiness. With an open hand mindset, you reach for goals wanting but not clinging to them, allowing them to come or go organically without stressing you either way.

Imagine you're reaching to pick an apple in an orchard. If you cling too tightly as you pick it, you'll likely bruise the apple. But with a relaxed grip using just your fingertips, the apple easily comes free unharmed. Goals can be handled in the same way.

Desiring Without Needing

The key is desiring your goals while simultaneously accepting not getting them and knowing that you will be okay without them. Picture reaching towards goals with an open hand—wanting them but not needing them.

This allows goals to come to fruition organically or not without stressing you.

For instance, say your goal is getting into your top choice graduate program. You've always dreamed of attending but facing rejection could be devastating. This fear causes attachment, tightly gripping the goal with anxious fingers. But by opening your hand, you want the goal without clinging to it as a necessity for happiness. You desire acceptance but don't need it.

Reframing Failure

The open hand approach reframes failures as simple feedback rather than crises. When you don't get something you want, it won't feel like the end of the world. You intended to pick up an apple, but it fell from the tree before you grabbed it. No matter. You move on, seeking other appealing apples without frustration over the one lost. With goals, you redirect this same calm attitude toward repeating efforts.

Preventing Self-Worth Ties

By removing neediness towards goals, you also avoid tying self-worth to outcomes. If you cling tightly to getting your dream job for validation but then don't get it, you may feel defeated as a person. But seeing goals as mere desires allows you to separate progress and reversals from your inner value. Even if the apple you reached for had a worm inside and wasn't palatable, it doesn't say anything about your worthiness; you simply try again.

Cultivating Openness

Adopting an open hand mindset takes practice and self-reflection. Start by noticing when you clench goals tightly in anxiety. Then consciously relax your grip, focusing on internal stability over needing external results. Affirm your inherent worth doesn't change with achievement.

When fear of failure creeps in, redirect your mindset to flexibility and persistence. Appreciate goals as optional invitations, not rigid demands. Over time, this mental reset will create calm spaciousness around desires. Your hands will unclench, ready to receive gifts appearing, but also willing to have them pass by uncaught. You will reach steadily, motivated yet unattached, empowered from within not outcomes. With open palms, you welcome life's bounty but do not require it to be whole.

Enabling Persistence

Finally, having flexible expectations of achievement takes pressure off so you can persevere. If you tell yourself an apple falling equals irrevocable failure, the weight makes giving up appealing. But without rigid demands, you remain motivated, knowing you chose goals freely rather than out of perceived necessity. You can shake off disappointments knowing there are always more apples to try for and that the missed one says nothing permanent about you.

Pursuing goals with an open hand takes courage, vulnerability, and self-trust, but the payoff is immense. It enables embracing life fully while dropping the crushing pressure of rigid expectations. You step forward boldly towards fulfilling objectives but face the unknown future without fear, come what may. Your sense of inner solidity remains unshaken by outer turbulence. You retain motivation amidst disappointment through self-belief, rather than being derailed by events outside your control. With palms open but presence strong, you remain stable through life's ebbs and flows, grounded in who you are, not what you achieve. This poise allows you to reach your potential smoothly.

In summary, pursuing goals with an open hand enables peace of mind. You act without angst, separate progress from identity, and persist flexibly. And this loosened grip means goals that do come to fruition will be that much sweeter.

The Light You Find in Your Darkest Hour

Finding Gratitude in Your Darkest Moments

Life has a way of testing us - throwing obstacles, challenges, and painful experiences in our path. When you're in the depths of hardship or heartache, it can be incredibly difficult to find the positive or feel grateful. However, embracing gratitude for even your darkest moments can profoundly shape who you become.

The Hard Times Build Your Strength

The hardest moments in your life will require you to dig deep, face your fears, and discover just how resilient you truly are. Without adversity, you wouldn't build the kind of mental, emotional, and spiritual muscles that allow you to weather life's storms. Difficult times force you to find inner reserves of courage, tenacity, patience and hope when you feel you have none left. They build your self-confidence and show you what you can survive.

When faced with crisis, failure, grief or pain, avoiding or resisting will only lead to more suffering. By meeting the challenge head on - shedding tears when you must but continuing to put one foot in front of the other - you move through the pain to the other side where you're stronger, wiser and more compassionate. Every difficult or dark moment develops inner fortitude. The challenges you've already overcome live on inside, helping you handle whatever comes next.

Mistakes and Failures Expand Yourself

Without failure and mistakes, you'd stay trapped within your comfort zone, repeating the same safe behaviors but only getting the same results. However, each misstep, each disappointment, and each wrong turn forces growth. Mistakes humble you when you need it most. They expand your experience. Failure gives you firsthand practice in letting go of your ego, getting back up again, and trying new approaches until you succeed.

Close the gap between who you are and who you want to be with patience and curiosity instead of self-judgment when you come up short. Reframe failures and mistakes as teachers pointing the way forward rather than rebukes calling you inadequate. Stay open to the hard-won lessons mistakes provide, then move ahead wiser. Each failure makes more success possible, and each recovered misstep makes what you ultimately create that much more amazing.

Grief Connects You Through Loss

The grief and sense of loss you feel after tragedy, death, crisis, or even endings like divorce or leaving a job behind work to open your heart. The pain of loss strips everything nonessential away so you can see others and the human experience more profoundly. Your defences and personal barriers naturally descend when grieving. This allows compassion and empathy to ascend in its place, connecting you more deeply with people and life itself.

By fully living through and embracing the grieving process, no matter how gutting it feels in the moment, you gain the capacity to truly be present with others going through similar losses. Your darkness grants you the gift of connection. After experiencing personal depths of sorrow or pain, you find yourself able to hold space for someone else's dark night of the soul. Through your journey to hope, you light the way for them as well.

You Are Shaped By All of It

Trying times change your trajectory. Hardship alters your perspective and priorities. Loss shifts your spirit. Without all the highs and lows - the joyous successes and the devastating failures - you would still remain incomplete. Gratitude, even for your darkest and most difficult moments, which felt unbearable in the midst of them, allows peace and lets you see how every piece shaped your life meaningfully.

Your life path reflects all of it - blissful, beautiful moments as well as shadowy seasons punctuated by pain. But just as winter's descent into frozen darkness heralds spring's return, the wheel turns through light and dark so you can live into your wholeness. Moments you perceived as mistakes or pointless detours circled back, transforming you. Hardships made you wiser and more humble. Losses connected and centered you.

Dark nights, storms, and even tragedy hold their own strange, compelling beauty if you stop resisting and instead open to learning. Viewed in retrospect with grateful eyes rather than the judgment, fear or regret you felt at the time, you understand now that every aspect of your past had to happen exactly as it did - the disappointments as much as the successes - to create the complete being you are today. For that, even past you can hardly recognize, gratitude allows peace. When we release the need to judge our past and instead accept it with gentle understanding, we find wholeness. The full tapestry of our lives, woven with dark strands and light, creates a work of profound meaning. We grasp that all we have experienced has shaped us, and so we make peace with our history, imperfections and all. This gratitude for the totality of our journey births deep insight into who we truly are.

Healing the Soul through Ho'oponopono

Clearing the Clouds of Yesterday

WE ALL HAVE REGRETS that linger - words uttered in haste, actions we wish we could take back. Like storm clouds, these unresolved hurts block the sunshine trying to nurture our growth. The Hawaiians practice Ho'oponopono to reconcile the past and make way for the future.

At its heart, Ho'oponopono guides us to take responsibility - to offer sincere apologies, grant ourselves grace, and release others from blame. As we acknowledge our shortcomings with compassion rather than shame, we lighten our spirits. The mantra **"I'm sorry, please forgive me, I love you, thank you"** cleanses away pride and resentment with humility and love.

This ritual opens our eyes to see those who harmed us as flawed beings like ourselves rather than enemies. It helps us recognize their context, motivations, and wounds so we can be free of bitterness's grip. We envision improved relations and brighter days ahead, feeling the emotional release as we let grievances go.

When we make amends internally and externally, we pave the way for inspiration to sprout through cracks where pain once divided us from others. We transform from victims clinging to our side of the story to empowered creators ready to manifest our destiny. No longer weighed down by yesterday's storms, we stand clear to invite magic into today. Where in your past might you still be carrying hurts that keep you from moving forward in full faith? Consider reflecting on any lingering regrets or grudges using the Ho'oponopono ritual. With an open heart, you can dissolve the clouds to let the light in.

Ho'oponopono

> **Center Yourself:** Close your eyes and take some three deep breaths. As you exhale, release any tension or negativity you're carrying. Clear your mind completely.
>
> **Reflect:** Look inward and acknowledge any regrets that still weigh on you - actions taken, words said, feelings held onto. Consider why others acted as they did, but don't justify harm. Put yourself in their shoes.
>
> **Take Accountability:** Offer a sincere, specific apology out loud or in a letter - admit where you were wrong and ask forgiveness. Then grant yourself grace, knowing we all make mistakes. If possible, apologize privately to anyone you hurt. If unavailable, write a symbolic letter. Or visualize a conversation expressing remorse.
>
> **Recite Relief:** Repeat the mantra **"I'm sorry, please forgive me, I love you, thank you"** - feel the emotional release with each phrase. Envision your relationships renewed and your days brighter, having released this burden. Forgiveness cleanses and heals.

Repeat this ritual as needed until you feel inner resolution. With an open heart, you can be free of the past's grip.

When You Outgrow Your Tribe

"You are the average of the five people you spend the most time with." – **Jim Rohn**

Outgrowing Your Tribe

We all start out in a tribe - a group we feel connected to and supported by. Your tribe might be your family, hometown friends, or a community you discovered. There often comes a point when we feel we've outgrown our tribe. The people who once brought comfort can begin to stifle growth. Their beliefs no longer align with yours. This chapter is for those looking to find their new community.

You May Feel Like an Outsider

At first, you may not notice the changes happening within you. It's gradual. You find yourself disagreeing with your tribe's views more often. Their once-entertaining stories now feel shallow. You've outgrown their activities and conversations.

You may keep these feelings private, but your friends and family may sense you pulling away. They react by tightening their grip, criticizing your changing ideals and interests. Confused by your evolution, they try to keep you where you are.

The more you diverge, the more isolated you may feel, searching for connection and understanding. You float in purgatory – no longer at home with your old tribe but not yet welcomed into a new one.

This loneliness weighs on you. You wonder if you should suppress your changes to please your tribe. But deep down, you know forcing yourself backwards is impossible. Your growth is inevitable.

Finding a New Tribe

Staying with a tribe you've outgrown can stifle your growth. When your beliefs no longer align, it's often time to move on. This doesn't necessarily mean cutting all contact. Many people maintain friendships even after outgrowing a tribe. But limiting time with them may be necessary for your evolution.

Letting go of your tribe can be challenging and sad. You're stepping away from people you relied on into uncertainty. But remember, this sadness is temporary. The joy you'll feel in your new community will exceed the brief grief of transitioning.

Seek out those who welcome growth, not resist it. Surround yourself with people who celebrate your evolution, even if they don't fully understand it. A supportive tribe empowers your journey wherever it takes you.

Getting Comfortable with Discomfort

Stepping outside your comfort zone can help you find your new community. Avoid complacency by continually expanding your horizons.

Pursue events that interest you, even alone. Talk to new people when traveling. Say yes to intriguing hobbies. Make an effort to meet people online and offline. Not every attempt will lead to new friends. Some encounters may be awkward. But the more you put yourself out there, the more likely you'll attract your tribe. Progress requires discomfort. Lean into uncertainty to reach unexpected heights.

RAISING YOUR VIBRATION

As you learn and grow, you begin attracting a new tribe on your wavelength. Focus within. Pursue knowledge and practices like meditation that bring you joy. As you raise your vibe, you'll draw in supportive new friends.

Pay attention to who you're attracting. Do they share your values and interests? Do they support your unconditional growth? When you find uplifting connections, nurture those bonds. Not everyone you meet will become your tribe. Look for those as passionate about evolving as you. Lift your vibe, and your community will find you.

YOU'VE FOUND YOUR NEW TRIBE

One day, you'll realize you're surrounded by your people. You've found a tribe excited to see you evolve. Your new tribe embraces you completely. You can be yourself without pretense. You feel understood, seen, and valued.

With their upbeat energy, your tribe inspires you to keep growing. Their unconditional support gives you the courage to reach unprecedented heights. Together, your potential is limitless. When you find your community, cherish them. Show gratitude for their role in your life. Offer them the same boundless encouragement they provide you.

Trust you're exactly where you need to be right now. Enjoy this sense of belonging. Keep evolving, and your tribe will evolve with you. A supportive community empowers your growth wherever it takes you next. Keep growing, and your tribe will grow alongside you. A true tribe supports your continuing evolution wherever it leads you next.

Chapter 14

GET CLEAR

Find Your North Star

The Surface Desire

It's easy to get caught up in the desire for money - the wish to accumulate wealth, achieve financial freedom, and buy whatever you want. But this surface desire often does not lead to lasting happiness. [1] Studies show that after basic needs are met, increased income does not significantly improve life satisfaction.

Money Isn't Everything

The truth is money alone cannot provide deep, enduring co. Focusing only on making money is limiting. It neglects core human needs for purpose, connection, and personal growth. You prosper more fully when you move beyond wishing for material wealth. Align your desires with your unique gifts, values and life purpose.

Know Your Motivation

Before chasing money, understand why you want it. What feelings do you link to being wealthy? Security? Freedom? Status? Power? Validate these emotions. But don't let money be the only solution. Consider how to create financial abundance while also nurturing non-material prosperity like happiness, contentment, and self-actualization.

---

1. https://www.pnas.org/doi/abs/10.1073/pnas.1011492107

The Journey Matters

Think of it like planning for an exotic trip. If you simply pack some bags and head to the airport without knowing specifically where you want to go, you're not likely to end up somewhere amazing. You'll probably waste time and money bouncing between random locales without experiencing their culture or sights.

However, choosing a destination like Rome infuses your travel with intention. You might study some Italian to better connect locally, visit ancient wonders like the Colosseum, sample delicious pasta, and immerse yourself in regional delights. Your journey now has meaning connected to this goal.

In the same way, understanding the deeper motivations behind your financial desires focuses your efforts with purpose and significance.

Just vaguely wanting more money leads to random, fruitless efforts that don't satisfy the real reasons it's desired. But by knowing your purpose - perhaps to provide family security, donate to important causes or fund a long-sabbatical - you direct financial energies toward fulfilling and meaningful outcomes.

This clarity of purpose focuses your mindset, priorities and actions - from saving patterns to career moves - toward acquiring finances in a way aligned with deeper personal fulfillment, not just accumulating cash. Your "why" behind wanting money gives the "how" of getting it significance and context to enrich your life's journey.

THE 12 UNIVERSAL LAWS

LOOKING DEEPER

To attract true wealth, look beyond the money itself. Dig deeper to uncover:

> **Why do you want financial abundance?**
>
> - What one thing could money change for you?
> - In what ways do you want it to stay the same?
> - How would it improve your life?
> - How would you feel if you had money?
> - How do you define success in your life?

FINDING YOUR NORTH STAR FROM WITHIN

Manifesting true wealth begins with uncovering your inner North Star – clarifying the higher purpose behind desired money and outcomes.

Quiet your mind through meditation or time in nature. With compassion, ask, "Why do I want more money? What deep emotional needs might it meet? How would it impact family, contribution, stability, self-worth?"

Listen as your reasons reveal what provides meaning. Beyond surface wishes for possessions or status, your motivation likely connects to longing for security, freedom to fully express who you are, or leaving a legacy. Discover what makes your spirit come alive.

Write out the insights surfacing. Let your North Star clarity guide you so finances align with meeting emotional needs, not chase empty accumulation. If family time matters most, consider career moves that provide flexibility, not just higher pay. If you're driven by service, research charitable foundations or volunteer roles to integrate purpose with profession.

As you follow your North Star – acting on inspiration without constraint – you build an internal reference point of truth. External barriers begin falling away when your actions serve identified purpose rather than rewards or validation. Financial gains then arise more effortlessly since you operate from inner abundance.

Of course, purpose and direction unfold gradually, not overnight. Remain patient with yourself, using nudges of intuition to course-correct. Over time, as actions increasingly mirror inner wisdom, your North Star glows brighter to illuminate life's journey.

Keep referring back to the discovered purpose when feeling lost or doubtful. Lean into this compass with faith, allowing your North Star to guide you through storms into the open waters of genuine fulfillment. The more you live your truth without apology, the more blessings unfold.

In summary, clearly know your deeper "why" and orient all decisions by this North Star. Manifest wealth through awakening purpose then courageously stewarding it. Allow who you are, not what you own, to enrich this wondrous journey.

Write your most important North Star below:

Dream without Limits

Dream Big

Y‌ou've likely heard the phrase, "Shoot for the moon; even if you miss, you'll land among the stars." Now, we are going to explore why you should embrace that motto when setting goals and dreaming big. The universe wants you to envision an extraordinary life, not limit yourself to ordinary outcomes.

Your Mindset Matters

Just as a sculptor visualizes the finished statue encased in a block of marble before making the first chip, you must see the fulfilled vision of your life before taking the first steps toward achieving it. The mind conceives what it believes to be possible. And when you believe in yourself, the universe conspires to make the extraordinary reality.

Plant Seeds for Growth

A tiny mustard seed contains an entire tree inside it, waiting to unfurl. Set big goals that might seem unrealistic at first glance. These ambitious dreams plant seeds of possibility that can grow into remarkable results. Limiting your vision limits your potential. You may not achieve that ultimate goal, but in striving for it you will accomplish more than you imagined.

For example, imagine you are an aspiring author, and you dream of writing a best-selling novel that gets adapted into a major Hollywood film. That goal seems improbable initially. But in working toward it, you dedicate more time to writing and honing your craft daily. You eventually self-publish an e-book that sells modestly but gets positive reviews. This small success and feedback motivate you to keep improving. A few years later, you land a book deal with a major publisher. And a decade after first setting that audacious goal, you walk the red carpet at the premiere of the film based on your novel. You made your dream a reality through small, consistent steps over time.

Tune Out the Inner Critic

That voice inside saying **"You can't do that"** or **"You don't deserve this"** is not an oracle. It echoes past pains and false narratives about what you are capable of. Drown out the inner critic by affirming your strengths and envisioning your success as vividly as possible. The universe responds to faith and vision with positive energy to support your efforts.

Nurture the Dream Over Time

The universe helps those who help themselves. Outlandish dreams rarely materialize overnight (unless you win the lottery!). Nurture your biggest visions by setting incremental goals and milestones. Break down that huge dream into small, manageable steps and celebrate when you reach them. Stay committed to real progress and growth over time.

Sparking Quantum Leaps

Sometimes the universe will surprise you with rapid transformations or "quantum leaps" toward your goal when you least expect it. Stay open and alert to opportunities that seem serendipitous. The universe may send you chance encounters, resources, inspiration or other blessings out of the blue. Seemingly random events can spark energy that fuels your purpose and passion.

Reframe Setbacks as Stepping Stones

Don't let temporary setbacks zap your belief in what is possible for you. The path toward any ambitious goal has twists and turns. Every great person has faced crushing disappointment and criticism at times. The key is bouncing back with renewed faith in yourself. Setbacks help you learn what works so you can craft an alternate route to your goal.

WHAT IF

Approach life like a child gazing in awe at the vast night sky – untainted by limiting beliefs about what you can or cannot reach for. The universe embraces purposeful, passionate visionaries seeking their highest potential. Your inner critic, not any external force, sets the ceiling on what you can achieve. Defy self-doubt, nurture stretch goals over time, seize quantum opportunities arising, and view setbacks as stepping stones. Dream without boundaries or fear of failure. True fulfilment comes only when you summon the courage to take risks and chase dreams outside your comfort zone. Every great accomplishment began as an audacious vision in someone's mind. Passion is found when you believe in yourself enough to try for more. Though you may stumble, the thrill of aiming high will electrify your days. Look back with pride for having pursued your potential. You have greatness within waiting to be discovered. Don't just exist – take that leap, speak your truth, and follow your passion. Risk everything to find it. The energy of the universe will rise to meet your highest visions if you dare to dream bigger and remember what if it all works out.

The Power of Clear Intentions

Why it works

Setting strong, vivid intentions tunes your frequency to start attracting exactly what you want. Intention setting focuses your thoughts, energy, and actions toward a specific desired outcome. This concentration of focus aligns you with your goals on subtle energy levels to put the universal law of attraction to work. Quantum physics shows our thoughts directly influence what manifests around us. Intention fuels that creative potential.

Get Clear on Your Desire

Choose one meaningful goal you feel genuinely excited about – don't just pick what you "should" want. This intention will be your focal point. Whether starting a family, launching a new business or career, moving somewhere new, writing a book, or manifesting an experience at your dream destination, get very specific about what you intend to create.

Why Writing It Down Is Vital

Recording your desire in writing further cements and amplifies an intention's power. As you write, imagine and feel what it will be like when this goal manifests for you. Writing provides clarity and accountability that lights up your manifesting potential.

In fact, research shows people who write down their goals and intentions are more likely to achieve them compared to just thinking about them. The physical act of writing triggers powerful vibrational energetics and signals to the universe you mean business.

HERE ARE SOME ADDITIONAL TIPS FOR BRINGING YOUR WRITTEN INTENTIONS TO LIFE:

Use present-tense, positive language: This signals completion to your subconscious mind. For example, "I live in my stunning new home overlooking the Pacific Ocean" or "I run a thriving yoga studio that overflows with joy, healing and connection."

Inject emotions, senses and textures: The more vividly you engage all your senses, the quicker your desires materialize.

Believe in the possibilities: Write as if anything is possible – you are simply choosing a preferred reality.

A SAMPLE INTENTION:

"I live in a quaint cottage overlooking the vineyard-covered Tuscany hills. I awaken happily in the sunny yellow bedroom to birds chirping outside my window. The fragrant scent of fresh bread and coffee from the cafe next door fills the air…"

Let the research-backed power of writing down your intentions ignite your inner manifesting abilities. Discover firsthand how clarifying your desires sets your goals ablaze with possibility. When you commit your dreams to paper, you tap into cosmic forces propelling you toward your preferred reality.

Of course, intention-setting alone won't automatically manifest anything overnight. Consistent focus, strategic action, and trusting the timing of the universe all play key roles too. But taking a few minutes each morning to set your intentions infuses your day with positive, creative energy and establishes the fertile ground for seeds of possibility to sprout and grow.

When you're ready, put these manifesting superpowers to the test! Discover firsthand how clarifying your desires through vivid intention-setting can align you with your dreams.

Where Attention Flows, Energy Goes

What We Focus On Expands

You've likely heard the phrase, "What we focus on expands." We discussed the Law of Attraction chapter earlier in this book. This idea that where our attention goes, our energy flows and what we think about grows in our lives is an immensely powerful one. Here, we will explore how this mental principle works and how you can harness it to attract more of what you desire into your life.

Your Mind Filters Reality

Your conscious attention acts as a filter for what information your mind lets in from the vast sea of sensory data around you. At any moment, you have access to millions of bits of information - sights, sounds, smells, tactile feelings - far more than you could possibly process. So your mind narrows and focuses your awareness on certain details, filtering out the rest.

You don't notice the feeling of your clothes touching your skin or the ambient sounds around you right now because your attention is focused intently on these words. This filtering process happens mostly outside your conscious control, based on ingrained habits and assumptions. But with practice, you can exert more intentional control over what you pay attention to.

Shaping What You Perceive

The things that dominate your mental focus start to dictate what you notice and experience around you. Have you ever decided you wanted to buy a certain model of car, maybe a white Tesla, and then suddenly started noticing that car everywhere? They haven't just popped into existence - your altered consciousness filtered them into your awareness.

The same process happens with non-physical information. If you constantly dwell on worries about crime, you'll notice more news reports about burglaries or attacks. If you obsess over financial lack, you'll see scarcity and struggle everywhere. Your inner world shapes what details in the outer world you let in.

Seeing What Aligns with Your Beliefs

Not only does your attention filter what information enters your conscious mind, but it also skews how you perceive it. The beliefs and assumptions you internalize over a lifetime become mental shortcuts your mind uses to quickly interpret situations. This helps you function efficiently, but it also introduces bias. You tend to notice, remember, and accept things that align with your worldview more easily.

For example, if you believe the world is a dangerous place, you'll encode more instances that validate that. Or if you assume you're not creative, you're less likely to notice evidence of your own creative self-expression. Your lens of perception gets colored. Your attention seeks out confirmation of existing beliefs.

Funneling Energy Towards What You Focus On

Here's where the "energy flows" part comes in - what you consciously register and reinforce in your mind, you unconsciously funnel energy towards through your actions, attitudes, and decisions. It's like a mental momentum.

If you ruminate on how lonely you feel, you'll withdraw from people and exude closed-off body language, likely creating more loneliness. If you obsess over a goal like getting a promotion, you'll devote extra hours working, networking higher-ups, and bringing your A-game to impress the boss, all propelling you towards that achievement.

The mental seeds you water grow. So shift your attention towards desired outcomes, not the lack or obstacles. Think "I am moving towards healthier eating" not "I can't seem to stop overeating." The former puts energy into forward momentum, while the latter anchors you to the problem.

INTENTIONALLY REDIRECTING YOUR FOCUS

You might be thinking, this all makes logical sense, but try telling that to my anxious mind at 2 am! Sometimes, our attention clings tightly to worries, fears, or frustrating obsessions beyond our control. Practice gently guiding it back.

When you find your mental tape playing old, unhelpful thought loops, pause and say internally, "I'm going to think about something more constructive right now." Consciously shift your attention to picturing your desired reality - whether it's accomplishing a dream, feeling peaceful, or seeing issues resolved.

It takes practice to intentionally redirect where your mental energy flows. Start small by catching yourself ruminating and refocusing on positive visions for just 5 minutes. Over time, you can build the muscle of moving your inner spotlight at will, not just through habitual reactions.

Attracting People and Situations That Reflect You

Here is one of the most magical aspects of the connection between attention and energy. What you broadcast outward through dominant thoughts and feelings draws more of that essence into your reality.

If your inner world feels abundant, you'll attract resources, opportunities, and people who expand that by treating you generously. If you exude kindness, compassionate friends, and experiences that resonate with that quality, you will reflect it back. External reality - through some combination of actual events and perception shifts - mirrors internal reality.

So, show up first as the energy you want mirrored back! Think generosity, act graciously, make decisions empowered by confidence rather than lack, and respond with empathy. You'll be amazed at how life shapes itself around your dominant inner energy. Where attention goes, energy flows. What you focus your awareness on grows. Point it towards your grandest vision!

The dynamic of outer experience reflecting your inner world directly relates to the "Law of Attraction" - the principle that like energy attracts like energy. Focusing intently on ambitions, visualizing desired outcomes, and immersing yourself emotionally in your ideal reality sets in motion an energetic resonance. This frequency then draws circumstances, resources, and people that vibrate at harmonious frequencies to catalyze manifestation in physical form. So consciously directing your attention kicks off attraction forces, activating the mystical but scientific law that corresponding energies coalesce. Where you place your focus, you place your request to the creative quantum field of potentiality.

Find Your Glimmers

Why Glimmers Are Important

THE PURPOSE OF THIS exercise is to gain clarity on what truly brings you happiness in life, what I like to call your glimmers. Remember, life does not have to be perfect to be amazing; it is made up of moments that take your breath away even in their simplicity. By finding your glimmers, you will illuminate the people, places, activities, and experiences that resonate most with your soul. When we get caught up in busy routines, it's easy to lose touch with our core passions and priorities. This exercise provides a compass to help you rediscover what matters most. Remember, if it makes you happy, it doesn't have to make sense to anyone else. This can also serve as a stepping stone to making important life changes and reshaping your daily existence to better align with your truest vision.

> If it makes you happy, it doesn't need to make sense to anybody else

Remember the simple things.

Life's true treasures often hide in simplicity. It's not the seconds that count, but the moments – some big, others mere glimmers. That morning's first sip of coffee, a book spiriting you away, the comfort of rain tapping on windows—these moments weave magic. A stranger's smile connecting us in shared humanity—no grand gestures, just simple

COCO FAITH

beauty. A perfect bite of favorite food, a gentle breeze, a laugh with an old friend—all hold power in their quietude, creating meaning beyond measure. These moments, often overlooked, house the extraordinary within the ordinary. They unlock life's inherent magic when we pause to appreciate them. Discover what sets your soul alight, those moments that elevate your spirit. For me, it's a stormy night, rain against the window, lost in a good book with my dog Tarka by my side. It fills me with gratitude and peace. In these simple moments lies the extraordinary. Embrace them, cherish them, for they hold the true essence of life. By stopping to appreciate life's glimmers, we unlock the magic that's been here all along. In the ordinary, we can find the extraordinary. When you know what lights your soul, you can easily lift your vibration by doing the things you uncover here.

FINDING YOUR GLIMMERS

To begin this insightful inner journey:

Set aside 20- 30 minutes where you can immerse yourself in the process without interruptions or distractions. Find a quiet space where you feel comfortable, take a few deep breaths, and clear your mind. Imagine waking up at the start of your magical day, a day where everything unfolds exactly as you wish. Consider these questions and jot down whatever comes to mind.

- **Where do you wake up?**
- **Who is with you as you start this magical day?**
- **What do you eat for your first meal of the day?**
- **What do you wear?**
- **Who do you connect with - friends, family, community?**
- **What activities fill you with joy and excitement on this day?**

- **Do you have alone time to replenish?**
- **How does your surrounding environment look and feel?**
- **What would you talk about if someone was actually listening to you?**
- **Who makes you laugh or smiles at you in a way that warms your heart?**
- **What do you smell or taste that brings back nostalgic memories?**
- **What music, if any, is playing during special moments of your magical day?**
- **How do you feel when you finally rest your head to sleep again? What emotions wrap around you like a cozy blanket?**

Gaining insight into your dream life

Consider these questions, jot down whatever comes to mind, and review your vision. What patterns, values, or themes stand out? Compare your reflections to your current life. Are there any changes you'd like to make or activities to prioritize based on what emerged? This exercise can serve as an insightful compass, guiding you to align your daily life with your soul's vision. It illuminates what matters and reminds you to focus on what has meaning.

Don't let this just be idle daydreaming. Revisit your notes periodically as a source of inspiration for manifestation. With commitment, you can reshape your life to better reflect your dreams.

Finding your glimmers is a glimpse into the life you're meant to live. By taking this contemplative inner journey, you open the door to deeper peace, purpose, and joy.

Once you rediscover these glimmers that spark your spirit, commit to integrating more of them into your regular routines. Life often sweeps us into auto-pilot, where we trudge through daily motions oblivious to delight around and within. Make the conscious choice not to sleepwalk but rather to awaken. Build little rituals that weave soul-nourishing glimmers into each day so your life glows brighter. Perhaps it's pausing mid-morning to sip your coffee with mindful reverence, dressing to express your style while working from home, taking a different route to appreciate unexpected beauty, or ending the day listening to a beloved song. These may seem trivial, but they sum to life vibrant with colour versus monochrome. Soon, you'll find yourself seeking out glimmers instinctively rather than having fleeting encounters. When your days overflow with these soul sparks, you inhabit your world more fully, richly, glowing with inner radiance that can't help but spill over. Your shine will inspire others to illuminate their lives.

Authenticity is the Highest Vibration

The Cost of Inauthenticity

Conversely, being inauthentic involves wearing a mask and presenting a false version of yourself to others. This prevents you from fully living from your soul's wisdom. It keeps parts of your being suppressed or hidden away out of fear of judgment or rejection.

Authenticity is not about being perfect or always having it all together. It simply means you are real, raw, and transparent with yourself and others. Even if you make missteps, you course correct by using mistakes as lessons to align back with your truth.

Why Authenticity Supports Manifestation

Operating from your authentic being is foundational for manifesting your desires. Why? Because your vibration largely determines your ability to attract what you want into your life. Vibration refers to the overall level of energy you emit through your thoughts, feelings, beliefs, and actions.

When you are fully embracing your true self, speaking your truth, and making choices aligned with your highest good, you emit a high vibration. You radiate an energy that magnetizes your manifestations towards you.

Suppressing your true self in order to please people or conform to societal expectations lowers your vibration. How you show up then becomes misaligned with your inner world. This incongruence makes it difficult to attract desires because you send out mixed signals to the universe.

Research confirms authenticity leads to many benefits that support the manifestation process:

Increased self-esteem and confidence: Studies show people who live authentically have higher levels of self-esteem and confidence. When you operate from self-acceptance rather than doubt or fear, you believe at your core that you deserve to have your desires show up in your life.

Reduced stress and anxiety: Trying to stuff down or hide parts of your true self requires a lot of psychological effort. This causes stress and anxiety. But when you can simply be yourself, you experience greater peace and contentment. Your calm mind state allows you to vibrationally align with manifestation.

Clarity about desires: Checking in regularly with your authentic needs and values builds self-awareness. This clarity helps you refine exactly what you want to create so you can manifest consciously.

More supportive relationships: Authentic people build deeper relationships with others who resonate with their energy. Having a strong community provides positive energy and amplification to boost the manifestation process.

Flow states: Expressing your true self allows you to enter flow states where you are fully immersed in meaningful activities. In flow, you activate right-brain creativity and tap into intuition to receive manifestation insights.

Synchronicities: Synchronicities are clues from the universe that you are on the right path. The more authentic you become, the more you notice serendipitous signs and guideposts affirming your desires are coming to fruition.

Overall, science confirms that operating from your most genuine self puts you in a positive, high-vibrating state that is primed for manifestation to occur.

How to Align with Your Authentic Being

Becoming more authentic is a journey of continually checking in with your inner guidance and making choices that are in alignment with your highest truth. Here are some key insights for aligning with your authentic being:

Let go of people pleasing: A major obstacle to authenticity is trying to meet others' expectations or do what will gain others' approval. Make the conscious choice to let go of people-pleasing behaviours that cause you to dim your own light. Remember, it's ok to say no.

Honor your needs and boundaries: Respectfully communicate your needs and set boundaries that honor your well-being. Know you have every right to say no to anything that doesn't feel right.

Release the need for perfection: Perfectionism causes you to suppress flaws and imperfections out of shame. Accept that you are perfectly imperfect, worthy of love exactly as you are.

Stop comparing yourself to others: Comparing yourself to others pulls you away from your unique path. Make choices based on what's right for you, not what you think will impress others.

Express your creativity: Engage regularly in creative activities and hobbies that light you up from the inside out. This helps you stay connected to your authentic self.

Spend time alone: Make space for solitude in nature and meditation to remove external distractions. In silence, you can hear the quiet voice of your inner wisdom.

Speak your truth with compassion: Practice expressing your truth while also holding space for others' perspectives. Maintain empathy when communicating authentically.

Release inauthentic relationships: Certain relationships may encourage you to stay small, sedated, or censor your truth. As hard as it is, you may need to let go of people who do not support your authentic being.

Forgive yourself for past inauthenticity: Perfection is not required, only your willingness to realign with your truth when you notice you have strayed off course. Guilt and shame only stagnate your growth.

Make self-care a priority: When your basic needs for nourishment, rest, movement, and sanctuary are met, your higher self has the resources it needs to shine through.

The more you nurture your connection to your inner wisdom, the stronger its guidance becomes until being authentic is your natural state of being. With consistency, you can get into the habit of living as your highest self and manifest greatness.

Final Thoughts

Full authentic expression will likely feel uncomfortable and scary at first. But the more you practice, the more liberating it becomes to align your outer life with your profound inner truth. Have patience with yourself and trust in the unfolding process.

By boldly yet compassionately embracing all aspects of who you are, you will manifest an extraordinary life. Living authentically grants you access to your highest vibrational state, where you call in desires with grace and ease. Have faith in your true self, stay the course through challenges, and marvel at how your manifestations will blossom.

Chapter 15

IT'S ALREADY MINE

Create Your Ultimate Vision Board

Crafting Vision Boards for All Areas of Your Life

Crafting vision boards tailored to specific areas of your life can be a powerful tool in bringing your aspirations to fruition. Whether it's your health, career, relationships, finances, or other facets, these visual representations can serve as a roadmap towards your desired outcomes. By focusing on targeted boards for each of these areas, you can harness the full potential of visualization and manifestation. From depicting your ideal state of well-being to envisioning career milestones, nurturing relationships, and financial abundance, each board becomes a canvas where your dreams take shape and serve as a constant reminder of your objectives. Let's delve into the art of creating these personalized vision boards to propel you toward success and fulfillment across various dimensions of your life.

Find Your Motivational Modalities

Discovering your motivational modalities can significantly impact the effectiveness of your vision board. Start by exploring what truly resonates with you. Consider moments when you feel the most inspired and driven to act. Is it when you're captivated by vivid images, moved by the power of persuasive speeches, touched by symbolic objects, engaged with detailed data, or immersed in creative endeavors? Reflecting on these experiences can help you pinpoint the elements that ignite your creativity and drive. By understanding these modalities, you can craft a

THE 12 UNIVERSAL LAWS

vision board that deeply connects with your motivations, speaking to you in a way that inspires and empowers your journey.

Select 2-3 modalities from the following ones that you connect with most:

> **Visual**: *Do vivid photos, colors, and images excite you?* Choose elements that clearly capture your goals through powerful visuals.
> **Auditory:** *Do spoken words make concepts click for you?* Play audio clips, mantras, quotes and affirmations in your own voice when looking at your board.
> **Kinesthetic:** *Do you need to touch and interact with physical objects?* Add textures, fabrics and tangible items representing your dreams.
> **Logical:** *Does organized data motivate you?* Incorporate stats, graphs, and metrics to logically track progress.
> **Imaginative:** *Does visual storytelling move you?* Use altered images, artful photos, stories and symbolic designs.

When you choose modalities aligned with how your mind best processes information, your board activates your natural talents. It becomes a conduit for your inner wisdom, creativity and drive.

Let your vision board speak directly to **YOU** by selecting the elements most aligned with you.

CREATING THEMED BOARDS

Crafting separate vision boards for each life area provides additional targeted focus and motivation. It also allows you to customize for maximum resonance in that specific aspect of your life.

For example, your career board might include more logical modalities like organization charts, skills roadmaps, and statistics to help strategize professional growth. Your relationships board could incorporate more auditory elements like love songs, quotes about connection, and voice messages to activate emotional intimacy.

Having niche-focused boards also enables you to immerse yourself fully in envisioning success and fulfilment in each facet of your life, from health and fitness to personal finance to creative endeavours and more. You can tune in to exactly the images, words, items, layouts, and creative expressions that speak to you about a particular aspiration.

Reviewing the themed board aligned to the part of your life, you want to energize daily allows greater clarity, belief, and motivation to achieve milestones in that area. You can observe how a vision in one domain often supports and enhances goals in other domains too.

Ultimately, thoughtfully curated vision boards customized to different life domains help you manifest desires in a holistic way across your whole life. You create the intricate mosaic of your best life by realizing dreams facet by facet through targeted focus and visualization.

HEALTH AND WELLNESS VISION BOARD

Suggested Modalities: Photos of an active lifestyle, motivational words, nutrition/fitness graphics, fabric swatches, and nature scenes.

Sample Items to Include: Pictures of yourself smiling, fruits/veggies, yoga mat, nature shots, affirmations like "I nourish my body and mind."

You could include: Recipes of healthy meals, graphs of fitness achievements, magazine photos of radiant people, course certificates for health training, fabric swatches from workout gear, screenshots of mediation app progress, calendar marked with self-care activities, images of immune-boosting foods, photos of active hobbies like kayaking, hiking trail maps, pictures representing maintaining work/life balance.

Career Goals Vision Board

Suggested Modalities: Images of ideal office, inspirational quotes, new laptop/notepad, business cards, audio clips.

Sample Items: Photos of professional wins, motivational quotes, items representing skills to gain, conferences to attend, and mentorship opportunities.

You could include: Pictures of leadership, public speaking, collaborating in meetings, charts visualizing career ladder, images of diplomas/certifications, specialized software, professional development books, graphics with skills/traits to develop, recordings of career affirmations, business cards for aspiring roles, images of blog/book ideas.

Relationships Vision Board

Suggested Modalities: Photos of loved ones, romantic spots, lyrics, wedding elements, favorite date outfits.

Sample Items: Pictures of friend/family gatherings, dates, travel plans, heartwarming relationship quotes, inside jokes.

You could include: Photos displaying mutual respect, listening, laughter and intimacy, tickets to workshops/counseling, books on communication and connection, images representing conflict resolution, handwritten love notes, relationship agreements, collaged romantic location photos, fabric from dream wedding outfits, DIY date night ideas.

Financial Goals Vision Board

Suggested Modalities: Images of dream homes, retirement, travel, abundance words, debt reduction/savings graphs.

Sample Items: Photos of desired purchases, trips, home upgrades, prosperity quotes, and charts demonstrating achievements.

You could include: Images of smart money management, fully funded retirement and college savings accounts, graphs tracking net worth over time, affirmations for prosperity, pictures of charitable giving, screenshots of investment apps, photos representing side income goals, and vision collages for home renovation projects and decor.

3 Approaches to Vision Board Use

There are a couple of different ways to use your vision boards:

> **Prominent Display**
> Keep boards for your current goals and dreams visible in your living or workspace. Seeing them daily will keep these aspirations top of mind. Replace and update elements regularly to keep the boards inspirational.
>
> **Periodic Review**
> Store your boards together when you are not actively working toward those goals. Then, pull out each board monthly or quarterly to review and refresh your vision in that area.
>
> **No Review**
> Some people opt to create vision boards and then pack them away without ongoing review. The act of making the boards imprints the goals onto the subconscious mind. For some, further review is not needed.

Try each method - constant display, periodic review, or no review - and see what works best to keep you making progress on your most important goals and dreams. The key is choosing an approach you'll stick to long-term.

Who is Your Alter Ego?

The Power of an Alter Ego

Have you ever found yourself hesitating to chase after your dreams because of those nagging feelings of self-doubt or fear? Imagine being able to access a version of yourself that is fearless and self-assured, someone who has already accomplished your greatest aspirations. This is your alter ego, the most powerful version of yourself.

Psychology supports this concept. Stepping into a role has a profound impact on our thoughts, feelings, and actions. Athletes tap into a focused mindset to maximize their performance. Actors completely dive into the depths of a character's emotions.

Creating an alter ego or persona can be a powerful way to manifest confidence and success. Well-known celebrities have famously crafted distinct alter egos to channel bold personas on stage. For example, Beyoncé embodied her alter ego, Sasha Fierce, to perform at her very best. The rapper Eminem portrayed his alter ego, Slim Shady, an over-the-top dark version of himself. David Bowie famously took on the electrifying persona of Ziggy Stardust.

You already have many alter egos within you that arise in different contexts, which psychologist Carl Jung called [1] archetypes. We all have certain innate archetypes that makeup aspects of our personality and psyche.

SOME COMMON ARCHETYPES THAT JUNG DEFINED INCLUDE:

> **The Hero** - brave, competent, noble
> **The Sage** - scholarly, wise, thoughtful
> **The Explorer** - independent, adventurous, non-conformist
> **The Creator** - innovative, artistic, visionary
> **The Caregiver** - generous, compassionate, protective

We tend to identify most strongly with a few primary archetypes, while other archetypes may remain latent or less developed. But we can consciously tap into our latent archetypes or develop them further to manifest goals and dreams.

You can also craft your own unique alter ego - a Manifestation Icon that represents you at your boldest, most charismatic, and most successful. This symbolic persona allows you to step into those desired qualities and channel them through performance, writing, or even your everyday life. Experiment with an alter ego that radiates self-assurance, magnetism, and empowerment. Through this creative process, manifest your highest vision of yourself. But remember the Law of Oneness; any alter ego is part of your true self. Use your persona to spread more light. By manifesting your highest self with compassion, you can powerfully follow your dreams while uplifting others.

The Advantages of Having an Alter Ego:

- Infuses your mindset with unwavering faith in your success
- Aligns your energy with your goals by raising your vibration
- Provides clarity whenever self-doubt creeps in
- Gives you the courage to take bold, decisive action

Who is your Alter Ego?

The moment of truth has arrived. Now is your chance to create your secret identity - an Alter Ego that will empower you to defeat all obstacles in your path. Choose your name wisely, for it will shape the very essence of who you can become. Let it resonate with qualities like courage, strength, and conviction. When you speak this name, let it make you stand taller. Let it echo through your mind as a reminder that you are bold and unstoppable. This is the name for the hero within you. Write your name in the box below.

COCO FAITH

> **WHEN TO CALL ON YOUR ALTER EGO:**
>
> - When fear or self-doubt creeps in
> - Before big presentations, performances, auditions
> - During high-pressure situations at work
> - When you need to be persuasive or influential
> - To inspire motivation or discipline
> - When making an important decision
> - To maintain optimism during challenges
> - To stay focused on your vision and goals
> - When you need to say "No."

By invoking your Alter Ego in these types of situations, you tap into inner reserves of courage, clarity and self-belief to follow through powerfully on your dreams.

Mantras as Manifestation Tools

Harnessing the Power of Mantras

WHAT IF REPEATING A simple phrase could help attract luck, parking spots, or any intention you focused on? Let's explore how mantras may help manifest small miracles in your daily life. A mantra is a positive phrase or word repeated frequently with intention and focus. Mantras help crystallize beliefs, desires, and energy into reality. Across spiritual traditions, mantras are used to connect with something greater than ourselves.

Setting an Expectation

When you regularly repeat a mantra, it's like setting an expectation for what you want to manifest, which imprints on your subconscious mind. Choose a short phrase that affirms the outcome you want to manifest. The more present and focused you can be while repeating it, and the more belief you impart, the more effective it becomes.

My Mantra Experience

I discovered mantras when I started saying **"perfect timing"** to myself when approaching busy intersections on my daily walk. To my delight, the timing truly seemed perfect! Just as I reached the curb, the light would change. This happened consistently, defying probability.

I tried applying **"perfect timing"** in other situations needing synchronistic flow. On morning commutes, in airport security lines, submitting assignments just before deadlines. It worked surprisingly often, though not every single time. When it didn't, I simply trusted universal timing and tried again later.

The Vibration of Sacred Syllables

In many spiritual traditions, mantras contain sacred syllables or sounds that carry inherent energetic vibrations. The repetition of these sounds, like "Om," "Ra," or "Ma," is believed to attune our minds and spirits to higher frequencies and intentions. Syllables such as these contain layers of mystical meaning and resonance. By chanting them meditatively, we tap into spiritual domains far beyond the literal definitions of the words. Feel the vibration of your mantra as you repeat it, allowing the sacred syllables to elevate your consciousness. Listen to any subtle reverberations both aloud and in silence. Repeating it becomes a ritual of communing with divine realms of intuition, creativity, peace, or whatever intention you set.

Other examples:
"I am (your name), and only good things happen to me" - for added positivity
"What is meant for me, is destined for me" - for peace amidst chaos
"This or something better" - for lifted mood and perspective
"Perfect parking every time" - for finding that elusive parking spot
"Health and healing" - for improved wellbeing

PROOF OF POWER

Of course, being open and observing life's synchronicities plays a role too. But personally, I've witnessed how focused mantras attract surprising coincidences and smoother logistics more consistently than **"normal."** It elevates your participation in co-creating your reality.

While the mechanism may be mysterious, the proof lies in your experience when you try it. Don't just take my word for it—experiment with mantras yourself, and always remember to say "thank you" when the universe answers your request.

Choose one for an intention important to you and write it in the box below. Repeating it daily with belief primes your subconscious and energy to align with what you affirm. You'll likely find **"perfect timing"** happens more often than chance.

Let me know how your mantra practice goes! Wishing you magical moments of synchronicity.

Turning Envy into Inspiration

Flipping the Script

Oh, that familiar pang and ache of envy. I know it well. The stab when your friend gets promoted over you yet again The twinge of longing when you hear about your sister's dream vacation that you can't afford The yearning when you see your college pal achieving such incredible success in music

In our culture, envy often gets pegged as a shameful thing the green-eyed monster rearing its ugly head. But what if I told you that envy, in fact, contains a hidden gift? Like a Trojan horse, it secretly carries insight that can ignite inspiration and profound personal growth.

By reframing envy as your inner compass pointing to your deepest dreams, you transmute struggle into fuel for your journey. Envy becomes not a destructive force but a guiding light. Let's gently unpack this complex yet illuminating emotion and explore how to harness its power. When channelled consciously, envy can lead us to our highest potential.

Understanding Envy's Roots

First, know that envy is a universal human experience. Even the most content and successful among us have likely grappled with envy now and then. It stems from our innate desire for growth, longing for belonging, and comparing minds. Envy surfaces when we perceive that someone else possesses something we deeply crave but feel lacking in, whether a trait, skill, relationship, or opportunity.

Common triggers include career accomplishments, talents, beauty, relationships, possessions, or lifestyle. The problem is not the existence of envy but how we relate to it.

> **Do we ruminate and resent? Or do we reflect and redirect?**

Owning our envy with honesty allows us to harvest the wisdom it holds rather than poisoning our minds against others or ourselves. So when you notice that familiar pang, take a deep breath, then lean into the feeling rather than turning away in shame.

NAVIGATING ENVY IN RELATIONSHIPS

Envy often intensifies in our close relationships since we constantly compare. It's easy to envy your partner's career success, your friend's social life, or your sister's looks and style.

Relating skillfully starts with owning your envy. Communicate openly when you feel pangs of insecurity or longing. Give your loved ones a chance to validate you and help uplift your spirit.

At the same time, discuss how to healthfully support rather than enable envy. For example, asking for constant reassurance or measuring yourself against them fuels envy's downward spiral.

Strive to celebrate each other without competition. Mutual love means wanting your loved ones to shine bright while also believing in your own light. Envy loses its grip when you deeply know your worth.

Illuminating Your Deepest Dreams

Though uncomfortable initially, envy points with laser clarity to our core desires. It instantly reveals where you feel unfulfilled and longing for more in your life, whether consciously or unconsciously.

Rather than judgments about yourself or others, view envy as your inner yearning calling out to be understood and manifested. What longing does this person or situation activate in you? Your envy is a compass pointing you inward.

> **To harness this, mindfulness is key. When envy strikes, pause and reflect.**
> - If I peel away the layers of resentment, what do I see reflected back that my heart truly desires?
> - What does this reveal about my deepest dreams, values, and purpose?
> - How can I channel this into constructive inspiration rather than destructive comparison?

Envisioning Possibilities

Once you've tapped into the dreams fueling your envy, vividly envision achieving them yourself. This is where envy transforms from depletion to motivation.

Your friend's successful business is proof that your entrepreneurial aspirations are possible, too. Their loving relationship is evidence that you can also have the partnership you crave. Their talent is a reminder of the potential in us all to excel in our passions.

Rather than envy dragging you down, let it lift your sights to what you are capable of. Use it as a catalyst to clarify and believe in your own capacity to succeed in that area of life.

When we view others as models, not threats, to our self-actualization, envy evolves into inspiration. Their light reminds us of our own. Their path makes ours visible.

Manifesting Your Goals

I know it's not always easy, but try to see past the envy and focus on what you truly want. Take some time to get really clear. Don't worry about how it will happen; just capture your desires. Then, we can break those big dreams down into smaller, more practical steps. I'm here to help you map out a plan to nurture your aspirations into reality. One step at a time, we'll get you where you want to be. Manifesting your dreams often happens gradually through determined focus over time. Savour each small win along the winding road. What matters most is your willingness to learn, grow, and believe in your purpose.

Becoming the Best Version of Yourself

Manifesting your dreams is not about measuring up to others or proving your worth. It's about nurturing your talents and pursuing your unique path with passion. Rather than envy, let gratitude for those who inspire you light the way. When we appreciate people who model success, it motivates us to become the best version of ourselves. Their accomplishments remind us that within each of us lies untapped potential ready to unfold. So keep your eyes on your own paper, move boldly towards your goals, and bloom into the person you are meant to be. The journey of growth never ends when we walk it with purpose and courage.

5-Step Exercise

It's understandable to feel envious when you see others accomplishing great things. Envy is a natural human emotion. The key is learning how to harness it as constructive inspiration for positive change.

> **When you notice envy arising, use this 5-step exercise to shift perspective:**
>
> **Identify the trigger:** Pause and reflect on who or what triggered the envious feelings. Get clear and specific about the external accomplishment or attribute that activated this emotion.
>
> **Look Inward:** Ask yourself: What desire or dream of mine is revealed by this envy? What do I long for in my own life? Dig deep to name the craving beneath the surface.
>
> **Affirm Your Potential:** Remind yourself that this person proves your desire is achievable. Their success shows it is possible. Affirm that you are capable of manifesting this too, in your own powerful way, with your unique strengths.
>
> **Get Inspired:** Reframe this envy into fuel for your goals. How can this person's journey ignite your own in a positive way? Let their example inspire and motivate you.
>
> **Take Action:** Convert inspiration into concrete short- and long-term action steps. Outline specific goals, plans, and strategies. Enlist accountability to commit. Address any obstacles and how you can overcome them. Put in consistent work fueled by inspiration.

Journaling about your reflections and discussing them with a trusted friend can help cement the learning and inspiration. The key is shifting envy into uplifting motivation to pursue your untapped potential, one step at a time.

Visualization

Mastering the Art of Visualization

The pioneering teacher of creative visualization as we know it today was Shakti Gawain. Her 1978 book Creative Visualization introduced using imagination, affirmation and mental imagery to manifest goals and dissolve limiting beliefs. Gawain's teachings draw from Napoleon Hill, Norman Vincent Peale, the Law of Attraction, and harnessing intention. By making visualization practical, she equipped countless people to manifest their deepest desires. Her work sparked a lasting interest in visualization principles and science.

Why Does Visualization Work?

Contemporary neuroscience has uncovered concrete evidence about why visualization manifests opportunities and goals. Studies using MRI scanning show that portions of the brain light up similarly when visualizing an activity vs. actually doing it. This explains why visualization feels real biologically.

Specifically, visualization repetitively engages the reticular activating system (RAS), which filters stimuli and directs focus to what your brain deems important for survival and achievement. With consistent visualization of a new career or desired outcome, you train your RAS to perceive related opportunities that can bring your vision to life.

Beyond conditioning what you notice in the outside world, visualization also forges new connections and strengthens neural networks related to the visualized activity itself. This primes your nervous system for smooth execution once opportunities do arise. It's why athletes, public speakers and performers use extensive visualization to rehearse their skills for optimal capability by the time they take the actual field, stage or platform.

In summary, science shows that harnessing imagination, intention and attention through regular visualization rewires both your neurology and outward energy precisely towards your goals. By immersing mentally, you transform biologically. This demonstrates visualization's immense power to recreate your reality.

MANIFEST YOUR DREAMS:

Find a quiet space to relax and center yourself. Take a few deep breaths as you repeat the mantra:
"What is desired by me is destined for me."
- Silently repeat this mantra to yourself as you visualize. Let the words deepen your trust in manifestation.

- Now, bring your desire into sharp focus with all your senses. See, hear, feel and even smell your goal fulfilled. If your desire is a new home, visualize walking from room to room. If it's a trip, picture the sites vividly. Make it as real as possible.

"What is desired by me is destined for me."
- What would achieve this feel like? Let the emotions amplify as you repeat the mantra several times.

- When ready, return to the present. Reflect on connecting with your dream. Trust that through intention and imagination, you initiate manifestation. Carry the mantra as your guide.

THE 12 UNIVERSAL LAWS

TIPS FOR EXPANDED RESULTS

- Vividly visualize at key times - mornings, before sleep, during breaks. Consistency rapidly strengthens neural patterns.

- Occasionally, picture your desire fulfilled from the observer's view. Watch yourself enjoying the results.

- Voice record visualizations to magnify effects through repeated hearings.

- Journal accomplishments after visualizing them. This energizes your vision and reveals action steps.

Studies confirm those dedicating at least 21 days to vividly visualizing intentions accompanied by emotions and sensory details report enhanced achievement of their goals across domains like athletic performance, academic success and career development.

The power is now in your hands. Through focused imagination, you consciously create. Wave this magic wand wisely!

Quantum Leaping Your Reality

Activating Possibility

Quantum physics shows that everything vibrates at different frequencies, influencing form and function. Your outside world comes from your inner vibration - thoughts, feelings, beliefs, imagination and intentions.

When your energy lines up powerfully enough with a vision through extreme clarity, conviction and consistency, it can spark a quantum shift. This blast-off jumps you into an exponentially better reality against the odds.

Examples are winning the lottery with 1 in 302 million odds, getting a book deal when you almost gave up on publishing, or manifesting an amazing relationship when you finally loved yourself enough.

These lucky strokes of fortune break limiting beliefs about what you think is possible. They show reality's flexibility to quickly and dramatically match your state of being once triggered.

Activating Synchronicity

Quantum leaps often show up as timely coincidences and chance meetings rather than explosions. You unexpectedly meet the perfect mentor, an Instagram post leads to new collaborations, lost keys reappear in a previously searched spot.

Though they seem random, these serendipities emerge from the field of potentiality when your energy summons them. They build momentum to unravel blocks, open access to resources, and weave miraculous new pathways aligned with your vision.

Trusting Possibility

Of course, the mind often resists these reality shifts. We explain them away as chance, feel unworthy of such grace, or recoil at quantum acceleration.

But confirming reality's extraordinary flexibility to match our being requires surrender - a trust fall into the cosmic web ready to catch us at new heights. When doubted, quantum support sometimes disappears, then returns robustly when chosen again with conviction, like a test of readiness.

Quantum leaps need faith in extreme possibility plus clarity of vision, purposeful action, and surrender of rigid expectations. This combo pulses at high frequency to attract profound manifestation.

Activating Your Energy Flow

I call this sweet spot vibration the internal superconductor - incredibly pure, coherent energy flowing freely through you to conduct miraculous manifestation.

When cluttered by toxic beliefs, hardened emotions, self-sabotage, hesitation or doubt, your energy gets dirty, inconsistent and scattered. This builds resistance, diminishing flow, like poor wiring. You must clean up your circuitry through inner work to become a pristine superconductor.

Actively purify limiting beliefs, integrate shadow emotions, cultivate self-love, embrace your wholeness, and know your worth. This expands your capacity to hold higher frequency, conduct stronger flow, and radiate coherent light. You become a magnet for quantum possibility.

Amplifying Your Signal

Imagine your vision's energy as a radio request to the universe. The clearer the signal - the more defined, bold and emotionally felt - the better the transmission. A weak, vague signal often yields little results.

Just as diet, sleep, and stress management maximize health, aligning emotional, mental, spiritual and physical planes supercharges your energy. Peak vibration requires holistic harmony.

Fortify conviction through spiritual connection and quantum science. Magnetize emotions with gratitude, excitement, and love. Clarify visualizations and repeat intentions. Embrace inspired action. Your vision's request becomes bold and clear - the volume dial turning up.

Sparking the Quantum Activation

At a certain tipping point when everything unifies - extreme clarity, conviction, coherence, consistency, surrender, signal strength, conductivity - blast off ignites!

Like a rocket reaching the necessary thrust to escape gravity's pull, a quantum burst transcends limitations and hurtles you to the next elevated stage. Possibility made form. Probability defied. Velocity unleashed. Perfect timing collapsed.

One courageous step combines with destined meetings to unravel obstacles, align resources and connections exactly as needed, and open the portal to radically new territory.

This quantum activation launches you beyond restrictive assumptions and suffering into actualizing your vision faster and more abundantly than conceivable. Linear expectations give way to exponential manifestation.

Riding the Quantum Wave

Once you experience rapid materialization on this scale, expect to observe it again and again as you nurture the energy flow enabling these downloads.

Through practising presence, acting from inspiration, and surrendering expectations, you notice quantum leaps rising spontaneously without force. You learn to trust and ride the waves wherever they lead.

Your key is staying plugged into source energy - not figuring things out, making them happen or controlling them. Let reality shape itself around your vision. When tuned to this flow, life becomes one thrilling quantum ride after another and awakening to infinite possibility!

Chapter 16

REWIRE YOUR LIMITING BELIEFS

The Power of Your Subconscious Mind

The Hidden Force That Shapes Your Reality

WE TOUCHED ON THE subconscious mind earlier in the book, but let's explore it in more detail. Beneath your conscious awareness lies a powerful inner force—your subconscious mind. Like the underwater portion of an iceberg, this subconscious realm lies out of sight, yet its immense strength and hidden currents steer the direction of your life.

What Lies in the Caverns Below

Your subconscious mind records everything you have absorbed since childhood, forging belief patterns from the sights, sounds, smells, feelings, and messages it has taken in. It is shaped by an accumulation of droplets—each life experience, message, and cultural implication seeping in and crystallizing within the caverns of your inner world over the years.

This unseen terrain beneath the waterline anchors your reality based on engrained beliefs about yourself, others, and what is possible. Some of these subconscious patterns empower you, channeling confidence, creativity, willpower, and strength. But others erect barriers around your potential, limiting your imagination and determination.

When Inner Worlds Collide

Friction builds when your conscious goals and outward direction clash with subconscious beliefs hidden from view. The tension between what you aim to manifest and self-limiting patterns can overwhelm you. Self-sabotage can even appear as your inner world rebels against conscious intentions.

To Harmonize the Two Worlds

The way forward is not to fight against this powerful subconscious force but to harmonize it. Through practices like meditation, journaling, affirmations, and vision boards, you can uncover unconscious beliefs and imprint new patterns aligned with conscious dreams.

Sculpting the Inner Terrain

By patiently yet persistently directing its flow, you can soften hardened thought patterns and transmute self-limiting structures. Give yourself permission to consciously reshape the caverns below through empowering visions and experiences.

Unleashing Your Full Potential

In time, outdated beliefs give way, so your subconscious fuels rather than inhibits your conscious goals. Its power is freed to manifest your deepest desires. You allow yourself to rise to your full potential by aligning this immense hidden force with your highest visions.

The subconscious mind, integrated at last, becomes the sturdy foundation from which you can consciously build, create, and attract anything.

CREATING YOUR REALITY WITH WORDS

THE POWER OF SPOKEN WORDS IN MANIFESTING

THE WORDS WE UTTER carry immense creative power. When we consciously harness the energy of our speech, we can profoundly shape our reality through the act of manifesting our deepest desires. Teachers across faiths and belief systems, from Napoleon Hill to Esther Hicks, emphasize controlling words to direct destiny.

Intriguing studies provide concrete evidence for vibration's tangible impact. [1] Japanese scientist Dr. Masaru Emoto performed experiments exposing water to different stimuli. Water exposed to uplifting frequencies like peaceful music or loving words formed beautifully intricate crystals. However, heavy metal music and negative emotional vibrations created distorted structures. The water's molecular structure directly reflected the vibration it was exposed to.

You consist mostly of water down to the cellular level. Like those water crystals, your cells are constantly receiving and responding to the energetic frequencies you immerse in. The stress hormone cortisol gets released when exposed to lower vibrations of anxiety or hostility. In contrast, higher frequencies like gratitude and inspiration elevate immunoglobulin levels, boosting immune function. Your dominant vibration literally shapes your wellbeing.

---

1. https://pubmed.ncbi.nlm.nih.gov/16979104/

Using Affirmations to Manifest

Affirmations, or the repetitive statements of intended outcomes, are commonly used techniques to manifest. As we linguistically affirm our goals as already existing in our lives, we program our subconscious minds to actualize this imagined future.

For example, rather than hoping for a promotion at work, one would affirm, "I am appreciated and rewarded for the value I bring to my workplace." The present tense imbues the statement with the resonant energy of current truth, which can then attract the reality to match.

Other popular manifestations using spoken words include writing them onto paper, reciting them in front of a mirror, recording them as audio messages, and stating them aloud during meditation. Hearing one's own voice repeat the influences reinforces belief and recollection.

The Mechanics Behind Spoken Words

Why do spoken words contain such manifestation power over merely thinking the same sentiments internally?

Several interconnected mechanics may be at play:

Vocal vibrations – The physical act of speaking creates vibrational frequencies that permeate out into our surroundings. The unique energy patterns of the words shape various cues in our environments.

Subconscious reception – Hearing the affirmations, rather than just thinking them, anchors them more firmly into the subconscious mind driving our habits and behaviors.

Quantum physics – Some theories point to quantum mechanics reacting to observations that "collapse reality" out of infinite probability waves into finite material forms. Speaking aloud manifests a clearer reality.

Regardless of the exact mechanisms, ancient wisdom traditions and contemporary mind-matter philosophies agree – those who control their speech can control their destinies. The words articulated with intention have the mysterious power to restructure our lives in the image of our imaginations.

Everyday Speech

It's important to be aware of how our casual, everyday speech can impact our ability to manifest. When we frequently say things like "I can't do that," "I can't afford that," or "I'm no good at math," we reinforce limiting beliefs about ourselves and what's possible. Over time, this habitual negative self-talk shapes our self-image and can become a self-fulfilling prophecy. By speaking doubt into existence, we energetically block positive outcomes and opportunities. Becoming mindful of complaining, judgments, and pessimistic language is key. Monitor your daily speech patterns. Are you vocalizing beliefs that disempower you or affirming your highest potential? Your thoughts do become things, so wield the power of words to elevate, not undermine. Make a conscious effort to reframe negatives into constructive phrases that uplift and envision the reality you intend.

Tested Applications

We only need to look to common advice across faiths, belief systems, and success ideologies for applying spoken words to manifest. Some examples include:

Mantras – Repeating simple phonetic mantras, both privately and in group chants, to manifest anything from spiritual transcendence to prosperity.

Vision boards – You can write down short key phrases that affirm your desired outcomes on your vision boards alongside relevant images and place them where they can regularly read them aloud.

Gratitude affirmations – Those practising gratitude tell others aloud how fortunate they are to have certain blessings already manifested in their lives, which then attracts more of those blessings.

No matter one's approach, manifesting with spoken words applies to all who dare give voice to their deepest visions and set them reverberating toward reality. The next time inspiration strikes, open your mouth and speak it into being.

Using Affirmations to Manifest

Affirmations, or the repetitive statements of intended outcomes, are commonly used techniques to manifest. As we linguistically affirm our goals as already existing in our lives, we program our subconscious minds to actualize this imagined future.

For example, rather than hoping for a promotion at work, one would affirm, "I am appreciated and rewarded for the value I bring to my workplace." The present tense imbues the statement with the resonant energy of current truth, which can then attract the reality to match.

Other popular manifestations using spoken words include writing them onto paper, reciting them in front of a mirror, recording as audio messages to play back, and stating them aloud during meditation. Hearing one's own voice repeat the influences reinforces belief and recollection.

While quantum physics and divine resonance may also play roles, vocal vibrations, subconscious reception, and observations collapsing reality wave functions help explain spoken words' power. Regardless of the exact mechanisms, controlling speech can profoundly direct our destinies if intentionally wielded.

The Hidden Benefits of Not Achieving

When Your Dreams Don't Come True: The Hidden Gifts

You've held a dream in your heart for as long as you can remember—one that fills you with purpose, passion, and possibility whenever you let your mind wander to that idyllic future. Maybe it's becoming a famous singer, writer, or actor. Maybe it's making an impactful discovery or starting a world-changing business. Or maybe it's something simpler but just as dear: starting a family, buying a home, or pioneering a new life adventure.

Whatever the case, this dream gets your heart racing with a thrilling sense of hope and promise. It feels destined like it was made just for you. And you've done everything possible to nurture this dream into reality—or so you thought. But somehow, despite your best efforts, that shining future remains out of reach. Instead of fame and fortune, you've been met with rejection and disappointment at every turn.

When Dreams Disappoint: The Protection of Limiting Beliefs

As much as it hurts, could your inability to realize this dream actually be protecting you? It may sound strange, but just below your conscious awareness, you hold beliefs that ultimately limit how far you reach to maintain your emotional safety.

These beliefs develop early in life to shield you from potential pain, failure, or embarrassment that your subconscious mind fears. At the time, the benefits of these beliefs seemed to outweigh the costs:

- "I'm not good enough" avoids rejection and feelings of inadequacy.
- "It's vain to want fame/success" prevents appearing arrogant or self-important.
- "I'll be exposed as an imposter" wards off shame and humiliation.

Though these beliefs limit you, your subconscious adopts them in an effort to protect your self-esteem and emotional well-being. They likely made sense, given your childhood environment and experiences. But what shielded the child now restricts the adult.

Replacing Limits with Love

The good news is you can consciously replace limiting beliefs with empowering truths:

- "I am worthy of realizing my dreams."
- "I deserve to succeed and be known for my talents."
- "I trust in my skills and preparation - any 'mistakes' are lessons."

This takes mindfulness, commitment, and self-compassion. But each affirmation reinforces your right to dream big and act on those dreams.

When you come from a place of love instead of fear, you give your deepest desires space to take root and flourish. You grant yourself permission to pursue your purpose and potential without self-judgment.

Unexpected Gifts on the Journey

Here's a beautiful secret: the journey itself holds unexpected gifts, regardless of the destination. Each step teaches you strengths you didn't know you had. Each stage of progress reveals insights about your heart's true longings.

You learn to find joy in the process versus fixating on an idealized outcome. You let go of the need for control and perfection. And you open yourself to possibilities that arise along the way.

So your dream may manifest differently than you imagined - or something greater may emerge in its place. Either way, when you commit to the journey, you discover you already have everything you need inside. The dream was simply a vehicle to help you honor the gifts within yourself.

Ultimately, the journey to realizing your dreams is about learning to have faith in yourself. Though the path may be messy, unclear, and full of twists and turns, you have to trust that you have the inner wisdom and strength to navigate whatever comes your way. Things may not always make sense in the moment, but often, there's a larger perfection at play that you can only see in hindsight. And while disappointments and setbacks will inevitably happen, how you respond to them determines so much. Can you let the unfolding be part of your growth rather than judging it? Can you separate your self-worth from any single outcome? Your dreams reflect the expansiveness of your spirit - carry that spirit with you through all of life's ups and downs.

Flipping the Script

The Seeds of Our Limiting Beliefs

Our core beliefs about money and self-worth often stem from childhood. While we had little control over our formative environments, the meanings we take from those experiences continues shaping our financial lives.

Reflect on your childhood memories around money. What messages did your family send about needs versus wants? Were certain comforts withheld, sparking feelings of shame for wanting more? Or did wealth ever feel precarious, imprinting fears of instability?

Consider the socioeconomic conditions you grew up in. Did the level of access and abundance available feel normal or inadequate? How did peers, pop culture or broader messages teach you what you could aspire to, and what was out of reach?

Many grow up hearing direct or indirect messages like:

"We can't afford that."

"Good people don't care about money."

"What makes you think you deserve a car/vacation/education?"

The young mind absorbs these words as core truths. Feeling unable to have needs met breeds resignation, while shame around wanting more leads to repression. We carry these deep-rooted beliefs into adulthood.

Scarcity mentality, linked with unworthiness, manifests in financial self-sabotage. We don't pursue that dream job or business idea because "someone like me" couldn't achieve that. Struggles feel inevitable, keeping us stuck. But by bringing compassionate awareness to these childhood roots, we can begin rewriting our stories. Those youthful conclusions about lack and limitation serve us no longer. Adult wisdom allows us to meet financial goals with confidence and conscience.

What messages absorbed long ago still reverberate as limiting beliefs? Examine them honestly. Then, begin planting the seeds for new beliefs of abundance, deservingness and expansive possibility. Keep nurturing these through daily affirmations, vision boards, therapy and other growth tools.

As your inner world transforms, your outer world will too. The key lies in courageously changing the inner narrative still shaped by past powerlessness. Recognize the child within; protect and provide for them at last. Let's begin rewriting your money story...

REFLECT ON FORMATIVE MONEY EXPERIENCES

Find a quiet space to reflect deeply on your past financial experiences.

Close your eyes and envision memories around money, going back as early as you can. Picture yourself as a child, teen, or young adult. What messages did you absorb about finances from family, friends, or society?

Did certain experiences make you feel guilt, fear, or shame around money? Were desires for wealth met with disapproval or punishment?

WRITE DOWN ANY LIMITING BELIEFS YOU UNCOVERED. SOME EXAMPLES:

> "Money is scarce."
> "Wanting more is greedy."
> "Money is evil."
> "My dreams are unrealistic."

Approach your younger self with empathy. The past is gone - you now have the power to rewrite your money story.

Create Empowering Money Affirmations

For each limiting belief, create a positive replacement. For example:

> "Money is scarce" → "I attract abundant financial blessings."
> "Wanting more is greedy" → "I generously provide for all my needs."
> "I'm unworthy of wealth" → "I completely deserve prosperity."
> "My dreams seem unrealistic" → "I manifest my goals with ease."

Recite these new affirmations daily. Picture and feel their empowering energy. Your mindset shifts as you water the seeds of abundance and self-worth.

Manifest Your Financial Destiny

Let go of past conditioning through self-forgiveness. You have incredible power to reshape your financial path.

Pursue work that lights you up inside. Tap into your unique gifts and unlimited potential. Your worth isn't determined by childhood circumstances, but by your own abilities and efforts now. Through consistent practice, you can rewrite scarcity into a genuine, lived experience of financial freedom. Watch your financial life flourish as you change your inner world. Keep transforming limiting beliefs as they arise. Do this with self-compassion - you are no longer that helpless child. You are the powerful author of your money story. Rewrite it daily.

> "Whether you think you can or you think you can't, you're right." - **Henry Ford**

Overcoming Limiting Beliefs to Unlock Your Potential

We all have beliefs - ideas and assumptions we hold to be true - that shape our lives in profound ways. Some empower and inspire us. Others restrict us and hold us back from achieving our dreams.

To manifest the experiences you desire, it's crucial to identify any limiting beliefs getting in your way. By bringing these into your awareness, reflecting on their validity, and reframing them into positive perspectives, you can dismantle the obstacles blocking your path.

Recognizing Your Limiting Beliefs

The first step is noticing when doubts, insecurities or self-criticism arise regarding your goals and desires. Pay attention to thoughts like:

- "I'm not good enough to do this."
- "It's too difficult for me."
- "I don't deserve this."

These reveal where your limiting beliefs live. Common themes involve:

- Feeling inadequate or unworthy

- Lacking confidence in your abilities

- Doubting you can handle challenges

- Believing you don't deserve success

Whenever you hear this self-talk, see it as a limiting belief asking to be addressed.

Exploring the Roots

Ask yourself: Where does this belief come from? Keep digging deeper until you unearth its origin story.

Often, limiting beliefs arise from:

- Past failures or traumatic experiences

- Childhood influences and conditioning

- False assumptions we've accepted as fact

"I could never start a business" may link back to a parent who disapproved of entrepreneurship. "I'll never find love" could stem from a painful breakup. By recognizing where your belief was born, you can start seeing it as something that served you at one time but may not be true anymore.

Assessing Their Validity

With compassion, take an objective look at any limiting belief from multiple angles:

1. Is this absolutely, unquestionably, 100% true all the time?

2. What evidence do I have that contradicts it?

3. What advice would I give a friend with this belief?

4. What are my strengths and accomplishments in this area?

"I'm not smart enough to succeed in my career" falls apart when you remind yourself of your proven track record of achievements, natural talents, and examples of overcoming challenges through perseverance.

"I'll always struggle with money" loses its grip when you reflect on times you've paid off debts, stuck to a budget or manifested unexpected income.

See beyond the narrow perspective of the belief. You'll begin to realize it was never based on truth.

Transforming the Narrative

Once you've loosened the grip of a limiting belief, start reshaping the narrative. Actively replace it with a positive, empowering perspective.

If you notice **"I don't deserve love and intimacy,"** counter it with **"I welcome healthy, fulfilling relationships into my life."**

Or if **"I'll never get out of debt"** arises, affirm **"I now experience financial freedom and abundance."**

Reframe the limiting belief into a new belief filled with possibility. Repeat it, write it down, and let it seep into your consciousness until it becomes your reality. This takes dedication and practice. But the rewards are liberation from old ways of thinking that have held you back for too long. You reclaim your power to manifest your boldest dreams.

Keep observing. Keep reframing. And keep moving forward as limiting beliefs lose their grip on you. With your new perspectives, you design your destiny.

The Cords That Bind You

Cutting Cords for Emotional Freedom

We form bonds throughout life that may linger long after serving us. Energetic 'cords' attach us to people, places, addictions, and situations - even past generations. While once nourishing, these ties can stagnate over time, draining us unconsciously.

Cord-cutting meditation helps energetically detach from what no longer sustains you. By mindfully severing outdated attachments, you reclaim your energy and power. This ritual practice brings deep peace and closure.

Understanding Energy Cords

Energy cords are invisible bonds that keep us tied to people, places, substances, emotions, beliefs or situations. They form naturally through relationships and intense experiences. The cords link our energy fields, which can be nourishing or toxic over time.

Imagine a phone charger plugged in, constantly supplying energy. Even after disconnecting, the charger cord stays full of energy until it's properly ejected. Similarly, our energy cords persist until consciously cut off. Stagnant bonds drain us until we sever them.

SOME COMMON CORDS TO RELEASE:

- Past romantic partners
- Family members or friends
- Addictions and unhealthy coping mechanisms
- Difficult workplaces or living situations
- Negative thought patterns or emotions
- Generational burdens inherited from ancestors

Trust your intuition on which cords may be stagnating your growth. Any relationship or attachment causing turmoil is worth exploring.

PREPARING FOR THE CORD CUTTING RITUAL

- Set aside 10-15 minutes alone where you won't be disturbed. Sit or lie down comfortably. Close your eyes and take several long deep breaths to relax into a meditative state.

- Visualize you're sitting in a room with a closed door. This room represents your subconscious mind. Ask your subconscious to reveal what person, place, addiction, belief, or situation requires cord-cutting for your emotional freedom.

- Wait patiently until the door opens and the symbolic representation of what you need to release appears before you. It could be a person, a situation or even a symbol. Your subconscious mind will know what it is and what it means, so just go with it.

Cutting the Cords

- When you're ready, visualize seeing the cord extending out from your solar plexus to the person/situation or symbol. Notice any sensations around the cord. Take time to observe how this stagnant attachment has made you feel - perhaps drained, obligated, angry or stuck.

- Then visualize yourself cutting through the cord, using whatever tool feels right - a sword, pair of shears, laser beam, etc. Keep severing until the cord fully detaches on both ends and dissolves completely.

- Feel the release as you cut this stagnant tie! Sense the burden lifting as your energy detaches from what no longer serves its highest good. Sit with the feeling of freedom.

Closing the Ritual

- Once detached, wish the person or situation well and thank them for the lesson as they exit through the door while you remain in your peaceful room. Take a few more deep breaths to integrate this release. Feel uplifted by your emotional freedom.

Regularly revisit cord-cutting meditation to detach from stagnant bonds still weighing you down. You deserve to feel energized and unencumbered by the past. Keep shedding what is no longer yours to carry!

Lunar Magic

> "The moon is a loyal companion. It never leaves. It's always there, watching, steadfast, knowing us in our light and dark moments, changing forever just as we do. Every day it's a different version of itself. Sometimes weak and wan, sometimes strong and full of light. The moon understands what it means to be human." **-Tahereh Mafi**

Welcome to a captivating journey into the enchanting world of lunar energies and manifestation. The moon, a celestial companion in our cosmic dance, holds profound sway over our lives. In this exploration, we'll delve deep into the mystical realm of lunar cycles and how you can tap into their energy for intention setting and manifestation.

Why does the moon matter, you ask?

Well, it's not just a celestial body; it's a powerful influencer of change, emotions, and intuition in our lives. This may surprise you, but our bodies, primarily composed of water, resonate with the moon's tidal forces. And during those magical moments of the new and full moons, the moon's gravitational pull is at its peak, infusing Earth with intensified energetic frequencies. Think of the moon's energy as a nurturing tide, ready to cultivate the seeds of your intentions. During these lunar peaks, your dreams gain the fertile ground they need to root and blossom. By synchronizing your aspirations with the moon's rhythms, you're aligning with the natural cycles of the cosmos, giving your journey a cosmic boost.

The moon's phases have been observed and honored by cultures across the globe and throughout time. Ancient pagan traditions used the lunar cycles to determine sacred rituals and planting seasons. The moon became associated with female deities and feminine power. Many pagan festivals coincided with full moons and were celebrated under its magical silvery light. Indigenous groups observed the moon for hunting patterns and to track the seasons. In astrology and alchemy, the moon became linked to intuition, emotion and the realm of the subconscious. Its cycles were seen as guides for inner work. The moon's energy continues to captivate mystics, Wiccans, and spiritual seekers who appreciate its awe-inspiring beauty and symbolic wisdom. By tapping into the moon's ancient rhythms, we reconnect with ancestral ways of engaging nature's magic.

HARNESS THE POWER OF THE MOON CYCLES FOR MANIFESTATION

By aligning intention setting and releasing rituals with the phases of the moon, we gain access to lunar energy that profoundly amplifies manifestation. Follow these steps under each moon phase to ride the waves all the way to realization.

NEW MOON MANIFESTING: PLANTING INTENTION SEEDS

1. On the night of a new moon, create a focused sacred space. Light candles with scents like lavender or sandalwood to promote calm. Lay out crystals like clear quartz, citrine and carnelian to amplify energy. Burn cleansing sage or palo santo.

2. Sit comfortably in your space with a blank sheet of paper and pen. Close your eyes and take five deep belly breaths to ground and center yourself fully in the present.

3. Choose 2-3 specific desires, and write them on the paper in vivid

detail. Describe how they look and feel already manifested in your life right now. Make them as tangible as possible.

4. Speak each desire out aloud three times, and really feel the words. Picture yourself already living this reality. Feel the truth of it resonating through your whole being.

5. Roll the paper into a scroll. With a candle, **safely** light the corner of the scroll and place it in a fireproof bowl. Watch as the flames transform the paper to ash, carrying your desires out to the universe for manifestation.

6. For the next 28 days until the next new moon, nurture your intentions by imagining them vividly each morning upon waking and before sleep. Take small aligned actions daily. Trust unwaveringly in the realization of your dreams.

Full Moon Releasing: Removing Obstacles

1. Under the glow of a full moon, recreate your focused sacred space. Light white or silver candles to represent the moonlight.

2. Sit comfortably with your eyes closed. Take ten deep breaths. On each inhale, imagine you are breathing in cleansing silver moonlight. On each exhale, release tension.

3. Settle into a meditative state and see the moonlight illuminating any limiting beliefs, stuck patterns, doubts or fears that may hinder your growth and manifestation.

4. Take paper and write down each obstacle the moonlight reveals, no matter how challenging. This brings clarity.

5. Speak aloud, "I now release..." as you tear up and discard each paper. Or safely burn them in a fireproof vessel to represent the release.

6. Chant "Aum" aloud for 2 minutes with focused intensity to amplify and seal your clearing. Feel the lightness.

7. Give gratitude for these insights.

By consciously planting seeds and removing obstacles in tandem with the moon's phases, your manifestation powers flourish exponentially.

Harmonizing with Lunar Rhythms

Intention setting and manifestation call for focus and action but don't underestimate the celestial influence of lunar energy. By aligning your intentions with the moon's cycles, you give your dreams a natural push, harmonizing your journey with celestial rhythms.

> The **new moon** ritual teaches the art of planting seeds when conditions are optimal for growth, while the **full moon** ritual reveals the weeds that must be uprooted for your dreams to flourish.

Engaging with the moon amplifies your trust in divine timing and the universal forces guiding your path.

As you become more attuned to life's ebbs and flows, you recognize them as part of your human journey. Through awareness of lunar magic, you gracefully ride the tides, intending your reality into existence, shaping your dreams into tangible, manifested realities.

The Magic of "Thank You"

"Cultivate the habit of being grateful for every good thing that comes to you, and to give thanks continuously. And because all things have contributed to your advancement, you should include all things in your gratitude." **- Ralph Waldo Emerson**

Gratitude is Magical

A simple **"thank you"** can transform relationships, health, and dreams. This chapter explores the power of practicing gratitude and provides a simple, daily exercise to manifest more thankfulness in your life. The Law of Cause and Effect is relevant - thankfulness ripples out, impacting all areas of your life in turn. Expressing thanks also utilizes the Law of Attraction, drawing more abundance and joy to you.

Begin practising gratitude by starting each morning with mindful thankfulness. **While drinking your coffee or tea, reflect on a few things you appreciate and whisper, "Thank you."** Feel the warm glow spread through your heart.

Throughout the day, look for more moments to express thanks - to loved ones, colleagues, or strangers. Feel free to keep a small notepad to write down things you feel grateful for. In the evening, reflect again on three things that happened or people you felt grateful for that day. Consider keeping a gratitude journal to write these down regularly. When you start actively looking, there is so much to be thankful for in each day – from good health to simple pleasures like a warm drink or laugh with a friend.

It's important to remember to say "thank you" to people who do small acts of kindness, like opening the door or serving you. Something as simple as holding open a door or bringing your food to a restaurant might seem like a minor thing, but it's still a gesture worth appreciating. The person didn't have to do it, but they chose to be courteous and make your day a little easier. Saying "thank you" lets them know you noticed and are grateful for their effort. It only takes a second to express gratitude, but it can really brighten someone's day and encourage them to continue being thoughtful. So next time someone opens a door for you or serves you in some way, make sure to look them in the eye and sincerely say, "Thank you." It's a simple act of courtesy that goes a long way.

Manifesting through Gratitude

Gratitude is a straightforward yet powerful way to use the Law of Attraction, the principle that thoughts attract experiences. Writing a gratitude letter to the Universe is effective. Make a list of all your blessings, big and small, including relationships, health, talents, nature, and possessions. Write a letter thanking the Universe for each item, describing why you're grateful. Also, give thanks for desires not yet fulfilled, which tells the Universe you believe you'll receive them. Imagine how you'll feel when they manifest. Regularly practising gratitude tunes your mind to abundance rather than lack. Expressing appreciation attracts more blessings into your life. Gratitude creates a self-perpetuating cycle of manifestation.

- **Find a quiet space and get comfortable.** Grab a pen and paper and let the words flow from your soul.

- **Start by thanking the Universe for all it has provided thus far.** Express gratitude for your health, loved ones, nature's beauty, talents, meals, and every comfort, big and small. This brings your awareness to the abundance that already exists.

- **Next, write about your dreams and desires as if they have already happened.** Thank the Universe for that new home, soulmate, career opportunity, financial blessing, or any intention you choose. Describe how you feel with deep gratitude and joy.

- **When writing, engage your imagination and all your senses.** See, hear, feel, taste, and touch everything as real and present now. This act of visualized gratitude uses the Law of Attraction to send your desires from the unseen world into the physical.

- **As you write with emotion, you raise your vibration.** This attracts matching energetic frequencies, activating the Law of Vibration to draw your manifestations into your life.

- **When finished, read your letter aloud with feeling.** Seal it and keep it somewhere special. Re-read it when you need inspiration and reminders of how abundantly blessed you are.

Remember that heartfelt gratitude is one of the highest vibrations. By writing daily, you activate deep manifestations through your resonance with the energy of thankfulness. Powerful magnetism occurs when your vibration aligns fully with the Universe. Continue writing words of gratitude to attract more of what you desire. Give thanks for all that fills you with joy, love, and purpose.

Chapter 17

TAKE ALIGNED ACTION

Be Like Bamboo

Bamboo Builds Unseen

For years, bamboo waits patiently underground, accumulating invisible roots each day without fanfare. Then suddenly, it bursts through the soil, shooting upwards at a remarkable rate of three feet daily! Bamboo wonderfully demonstrates the immense power of small, consistent action.

Just as bamboo builds an unseen root system to support mighty future growth, we must nurture our highest ambitions through regular tiny steps - the shaky morning stretches, the quiet journaling, the awkward first attempts. Do not ignore these efforts, no matter how minor they may seem! They are strengthening your foundation so that one day soon, you'll be ready to rocket towards your dreams.

Yesterday is but a memory and tomorrow is only a dream, but today, well lived, makes yesterday a memory of happiness and tomorrow a vision of hope. Focus not on the past that's gone or the future not yet here, but make the most of this moment, for today is the day to take action and pursue your dreams.

Remember - no one is coming to push you or do the work for you. It's up to you alone to make it happen. Success takes self-motivation and discipline to get out of bed and put in the effort day after day. When you feel like giving up or coasting on autopilot, dig deep to find your resolve. The only way forward is through.

Let's uncover the magic of "micro-actions" with an example most ambitious humans can relate to - establishing a healthy fitness routine.

Imagine it's January 2nd, and in a moment of inspiration, you set the scary big goal to "become really fit". Easy to say, but tough to transform this noble proclamation into reality, right?!

Here is where most people derail themselves. They expect to accomplish too much too fast, overload their schedules, exhaust their willpower, lose steam and ultimately quit after a few weeks.

Consistency Trumps Intensity

The key is much simpler: start embarrassingly small. We're talking mini-actions so easy they seem ridiculous. For fitness, that might mean: **"I will walk around my neighborhood for 5 minutes daily this week."** That's IT! **Consistency supersedes intensity.** By sticking to these micro-actions, you slowly start constructing the root system (a habit!) to support you over the long haul.

The Power of Tiny Gains

As you consistently act on your micro-commitments, you build confidence through tiny wins. Maybe after a few weeks, you will feel ready to upgrade, and now you will pledge: **"I will walk for 10 minutes daily."**

Celebrate these small gains! They are the stepping stones paving your path to remarkable achievements over time. After several months of regular short walks, suddenly, you might feel inspired to start jogging.

See how the mini-actions built an essential foundation? By being patient and avoiding the temptation to rush ahead too quickly, you created sustainable momentum. By sticking to these micro-actions, you slowly start constructing the root system (a habit!) to support you over the long haul.

Stay Encouraged Along the Way

When working towards ambitious goals, it's normal sometimes to feel discouraged or question if you'll ever achieve them. That's when consistency matters most!

Remember that you cannot see the complex root system expanding underground before the bamboo bursts upwards. But have faith it is developing each day. Likewise, the micro-actions you are taking now are slowly transforming you into the person capable of accomplishing your biggest dreams.

So when motivation wanes, reflect on how far you've already come, thanks to your regular tiny habits. Reconnect to why your goal matters and the benefits it will bring. Then, simply focus on the next small step ahead of you.

The Compounding Effect Over Time

Like bamboo, humans thrive on the compound effect - what happens when small changes repeatedly and consistently stack up to exponential results?

A 1% daily improvement in any endeavor adds up tremendously over months and years without appearing as though much is happening on a daily basis. But keep nurturing your roots.

While breaking big goals into mini-actions can seem trivial in the moment, forming and keeping these small habits inevitably enables outstanding achievement over the long run.

Just as bamboo ultimately towers into a mighty tree, you too can reach tremendous heights through steady micro-progress! So believe in the power you are cultivating through simple, consistent action.

"If you don't take action, you will end up paying rent to someone that did."

The Voice that Whispers to You

The Weight of Unmade Choices

L IFE IS FILLED WITH difficult decisions. Some are small, like what to have for dinner. Others are big, like whether to take a new job or move to a new city. While choosing can feel burdensome, often the heaviest things we carry are not the choices we make but those we leave unmade. Here, we discuss how to follow your gut when facing tough choices to avoid the regret and uncertainty of roads not taken.

Listen to Your Intuition

We've all experienced that feeling in the pit of our stomach when facing a big decision. That instinctive reaction is your intuition - your inner wisdom that senses what's right for you. Intuition arises from your subconscious, which holds a lifetime of experiences, insights, and instincts you've accumulated. It sees things your conscious mind misses.

When you have a choice to make, tune into your intuition. What does your gut say? If one option gives you a sense of excitement or rightness, and another fills you with dread, listen. Don't override your intuition with logic or practical reasons. Trust that it knows important things your conscious mind does not.

SIT WITH THE FEELING

Intuition speaks to us through our feelings and senses. A coherent mental pro and con list can actually override our subtler instincts. When facing a tough call, sit with the feeling each option evokes rather than analyzing the decision intellectually right away.

Notice where you feel tension or expansion in your body. Does one choice make your shoulders tighten and your stomach knot? Does another make you feel open and relaxed? Make space for your intuition to emerge before getting lost in analysis. The clearer the feeling, the louder your inner wisdom is speaking.

VISUALIZE THE OUTCOMES

Intuition works through imagination. To amplify your gut instincts, visualize how each outcome would feel if you followed that path. Imagine living each scenario in detail, tapping into the emotions that arise.

If visualizing one choice fills you with energy and excitement, even at the thought of the challenges it poses, that's a good sign. If another leaves you feeling empty or anxious despite seeming sensible, pay attention. Your gut knows which possibilities align with your fulfillment.

THINK OUT LOUD

Verbalizing your dilemma out loud to yourself or a trusted confidant can help clarify your intuitions. As you talk through the options and how you feel about each one, listen for where your energy and excitement come from. What possibilities light you up when you describe them?

You'll also get insight from putting things into words. Does one choice make sense logically but not feel right deep down? Does an option that seemed rash at first feel truer and more alive as you speak it? Verbal processing helps integrate gut feelings with conscious reasoning.

List the Pros and Cons

While deciding purely based on pros and cons can override your intuition, listing them can help give your gut wisdom space to arise. Write out the practical pros and cons of each choice, then sit with the lists and see how you feel.

Your intuition may draw you to an option that seems impractical on paper. Or you may find yourself feeling drained and dreading the seemingly sensible choice. Use the logical information to supplement, not replace, your gut read on the situation.

Consider the Consequences

Think through the long-term consequences of each path, both positive and negative. Not just the immediate results, but how they might ripple out over months and years.

Will one option align with your goals and values long-term, even if the short-term outcome is less certain? Will another choice provide instant gratification but leave you unfulfilled later? Considering distant consequences illuminates which intuitions to trust.

Sleep on It

When possible, resist making a major decision when you feel rushed, stressed, or otherwise uncentered. Your intuition speaks to you most clearly when you're calm and focused. If you can, give yourself time and space to sit with the choice.

Notice any new perspectives or instincts that come as you sleep on it take a walk or engage in activities that settle your mind. Silencing the static of stress quiets your inner wisdom. Give yourself mental space so your gut feelings can bubble up.

Choose Courage Over Fear

Growth and fulfillment often lie on the other side of fear. When your intuition points you toward a choice that scares you but also excites you, that's a sign you're headed where you need to go. If a safer, easier option leaves you feeling deflated, that's your gut urging you to be brave.

Trust instincts that align with your purpose and values, not just apparent comfort. Remember that fear signifies you're about to grow. Choosing courage over complacency will lead to a life without regrets.

Go with Your Gut

When facing difficult crossroads, the decision often becomes clear if you listen to your inner wisdom. By tuning into your instincts and imagination, you can hear signals that your conscious mind misses. There are no absolute rules, but trusting your gut will steer you true more often than not.

Quieting fear and hesitation allows your intuition to come through clearly. If you feel called to take a leap into the unknown, don't let fear hold you back. Life opens up when you have the courage to follow your gut, even and especially when the path looks unclear. What feels right in your soul is usually exactly where you're meant to go.

Chapter 18

LOOKING FOR GUIDANCE

Ask

The Power of Asking

WE OFTEN FEEL LOST or unsure of our path. Seeking guidance from a higher power can provide comfort, clarity, and a sense that we are not alone on our journey. By opening up and asking for signs, we allow the spiritual realm to communicate with us in profound ways.

Here, we will explore simple practices for soliciting and understanding guidance from angels, spirit guides, and the Universe itself. By leaning into our intuition and paying attention, we begin to build a powerful relationship with forces beyond the physical world.

Getting Clear on What You Need

The first step is getting very clear on what type of guidance would be helpful. Do you need support making a life decision? Are you seeking a sign to confirm you're on the right path? Take a moment to write down your specific request. The clearer you are, the easier it is for spiritual messengers to reach you.

Timescale

When asking for guidance, it can be helpful to set a timeframe for receiving your sign. This gives the spiritual realm a window to work within. For example, you may ask, "Please give me a sign in the next 24 hours that I'm on the right path." Or you can say, "Over the course of this week, please send me signs to guide my decision."

Setting a timescale creates space for trust and surrender. You've put your request out there and can now relax, paying attention but without attachment to the timing. Signs will arrive in perfect divine timing. Setting a general window simply allows you to tune in during a specific period. But know that guidance may come days or even weeks later when you are ready to receive the message. Be open and alert, but don't get frustrated if signs don't arrive within your set timeframe. They will come at the right moment.

> You can decide on a unique sign, one that is deeply meaningful and cannot be confused - for example, seeing a purple feather, hearing a special song, or seeing a particular animal over the next 48 hours. This specificity allows the Universe to send you custom communication.

OPENING UP THE CHANNELS

Next, you simply ask! There is no special language required. Talk to your guides, angels, and the Universe like you would a close friend. Share what guidance you need and that you are ready to receive signs. You can ask out loud or in your mind. Both are effective. The most important step is putting out the intention clearly. It may feel silly at first, but your higher self and guides are always listening, waiting for you to invite their presence into your human experience.

NOTICING THE MAGIC

Once you have put out a request, pay close attention! Notice feelings, songs on the radio, symbols, animals, unusual events - anything that catches your attention. This is how spirit communicates!

THE 12 UNIVERSAL LAWS

> Signs often show up in **threes**, so if you see or hear something more than once, tune in. Ask, **"Is this my sign?"** Check-in with how you feel emotionally. Goosebumps, tingling, warmth, and tears are all bodily clues that a sign is landing.

Over time and with practice, the connection will strengthen. You may receive full sentences in your mind's eye or crystal-clear knowledge of what step to take next. For now, enjoy the mystery, synchronicity and comfort of guidance flowing just for you.

DECIPHERING THE GUIDANCE

Once you receive a sign, it is important to interpret the message it carries. Pause and reflect deeply on what each sign means to you. Your emotional reaction offers clues. Pay attention to any goosebumps, tingling, warmth, or tears - your intuition speaks through your body. You may receive direct inner knowledge about how to apply the guidance. Or the meaning may unfold gradually over hours or days. Don't worry about analyzing - just sit with the sign and its energy.

Signs often communicate in metaphors. For example, seeing a deer could represent gentleness, grace, and natural beauty. Hearing an owl hoot may signal wisdom, insight, or the need to look deeper. Seeing 1111 on the clock could mean a new beginning is on the horizon. Have faith in your own interpretations, even if the meaning isn't obvious at first. The most important step is noticing each sign and opening up to receive the message. In time, you will develop fluency in this spiritual language just for you.

Angel Numbers: The Universe's Secret Code

Noticing the Signs

YOU KEEP SEEING THE same numbers over and over – on license plates, receipts, billboards. The sequences 1111, 444, and 555 seem to follow you everywhere lately. At first, you think it's just coincidence, but the frequency feels unusual, almost supernatural. You wonder, could these be more than just random numbers? Could they hold some deeper meaning?

Decoding the Message

Then you learn - these repeating number sightings are called angel numbers. Numerologists believe angels send us these number sequences as coded messages to offer guidance, reassurance, or validation that we're on the right path. Much like a navigation system recalculating a route, angel numbers signify course corrections and confirmation from divine messengers saying, "We see you and are here to help."

Each number sequence carries a unique meaning. For example, 555 indicates big change is coming, and it's time to embrace transformation. 1111 suggests fresh starts, new beginnings, and renewed alignment with your true purpose. 444 invites you to pay closer attention - heighten awareness, and tune in to the guidance all around you.

Angel numbers are said to appear more frequently during major life transitions or when we seek connection with the divine. They remind us the Universe is listening and speaking back when we ask for help. Their guidance empowers our intuition.

Interpreting the Code

You realize each sighting of 444, 777, or 1111 is an opportunity to pause, center yourself, and tune in. Ask yourself in the moment: What do I need guidance on? Then, quiet your mind, listen to your intuition, and pay attention to any inner wisdom arising.

Write down the numbers you see frequently and what emotional state you're in during each sighting. Notice any common worries, questions, or blockages coming up. See if interpreting the numbers' meanings illuminates an answer.

For example, seeing 555 amidst career uncertainty may signal it's time to release stagnancy and lean into another growth direction. Use angel numbers as street signs - they point you to where to go next on your life journey. Each one says "You're being divinely guided, keep following the internal compass of your heart."

Manifesting Meaning

Angel numbers find their unique meaning based on what you need to hear. Their coded messages help you tune in to manifest your boldest dreams. This guidance becomes a secret weapon, reassuring you that you possess inherent wisdom, creativity, and power. You're never lost or alone.

Ultimately, divine messengers only remind you that you're on the right path. So when angel numbers appear, see them as the Universe gifting you courage, comfort, and confirmation. Then, watch new possibilities unfold...

COCO FAITH

> **What special numbers/signs do you see recurring in your life?**

When you see repeating numbers, it's the Universe giving you a big, warm hug. These angel numbers are a way of saying, "We've got your back!". Breathe deeply and feel supported, even when life is uncertain. The numbers remind you that you have inner wisdom to guide you. You don't have to figure everything out alone. Keep following what feels right in your heart. The messages behind the numbers will become clear in time. For now, know that you're on the right path meant just for you. You've got angels all around, reassuring you that beautiful things are ahead. So take comfort each time those number sequences pop up. The Universe is simply saying, "We're here for you. You've got this!"

Akashic Records

Discovering The Akashic Library Within You

YOU MAY FIND THIS a little hard to believe without proof, but why not give it a shot? Let's explore the idea of an Akashic Library within you together. According to myth and spirituality, we each have access to a vast cosmic library encoded in our souls, containing all knowledge - past, present, and future. If true, just imagine what this could mean! By tuning into this profound realm of inner wisdom, you could gain incredible clarity about your purpose, guide your growth, and empower your manifestations. I know it sounds far out, but staying open and giving it a chance could lead you to discover amazing depths within. So come with me on this journey - let's see if we can unlock the doors to your own Akashic Library.

Your Internal Library

Picture your inner awareness as a grand library structured just like the ancient Library of Alexandria - Filled with scrolls, books, and manuscripts holding eternal truths. Each volume overflows with insights about your talents, relationships, direction, and any question you could ask. This boundless inner sanctum revealing your highest potential is known as the Akashic Records. Spiritual traditions like Hinduism first named this phenomenon "Akasha" imagining the universes wisdom written into the ether. Yogis, monks, shamans, and metaphysicians have accessed these records through deep meditation for millennia, emerging with revolutionary ideas. You can learn to tap into the records too.

- **Set Your Intention** - Approach with clear questions, just as you would research at a library. "What guidance around specific relationships, creative barriers, bad habits, or life purpose do you seek?

- **Quiet External Noise** - Find a serene space without disruptions. Dim lighting and play meditative music. "lose your eyes and breathe slowly to settle your body and mind. Repeat an uplifting mantra like "I am open and receiving wisdom from within."

- **Ask For Assistance** - Mentally request help from the records cosmic librarian who organizes this space. Imagine a guide - human, angelic, or animal form - who can direct you to the perfect book stacks. Tell them your intention so they retrieve books holding custom-tailored answers.

- **Open Your Book** - Understand that knowledge may reveal itself in many forms - as symbols, direct yes or no answers, illuminating quotes, vivid images, or simply a deep sense of inner knowing. Easy attention to the details and intuition you receive. Turn the pages slowly, allowing time for full comprehension. If a page is blank, pause patiently for the cosmic wisdom to fill in.

- **Track Synchronous Symbols** - Easy attention to any imagery, words, or ideas that repeatedly surface when accessing this place, just as library call numbers direct you through stacks. Keep a journal handy to record messages you receive. Trust that your unique symbolic language will soon feel coherent.

Take Action

Once you discover profound insights from the records about your next steps, digest how to practically apply that wisdom in tangible ways. Scribble action steps into your journal before returning from meditation so you remember. For example, if visions point towards writing a book - schedule time for research and outlining. If a relationship dynamic becomes clearer - have a dialogue with that person to improve communication. Anchor heavenly messages into earthly efforts. Know that you can always come back to these records whenever needed.

Consistent Access Unlocks Manifestation

Like a library card granting unlimited access to books, routinely connecting with your inner Akashic Records builds familiarity with this font of higher guidance to fuel your growth. "what could manifest from having an infinite resource of spiritual wisdom within you? Set the intention today to start visiting regularly.

What Rejection Teaches Us

Bouncing Back from Rejection and Self-Doubt

We've all faced our share of rejection, abandonment or criticism that initially left us feeling defeated. Yet the most successful people learned to let rejection strengthen rather than stop them. With time, you can too. Here, we discuss how we can use pain as power and build unassailable confidence from the inside out.

My First 1-Star Review

I felt like a failure when my book earned its first 1-star review: "Utter rubbish, a waste of money." After months of late-night writing around my day job, these few words stung worse than any punch. I wanted to retreat and lick my wounds; my motivation drained.

Yet, as I read forums, every well-known author had withstood their own barrage of criticism. I had two choices: let insensitive words derail my next book or pick myself up stronger. My dreams mattered enough to try again. You cannot control others' opinions. But you can control how much power they wield over your self-belief.

Over time, bad reviews bothered me less, and good reviews elated me less. I wrote because I had stories needing to be told. That required developing resilience when some would inevitably dislike my style. The confidence to create comes from within, not without.

A Child's Heartbreak: Abandoned by My Father

At age 10, my father abandoned our family. His sudden absence left a painful void where unconditional love once resided. I felt hollow and unlovable, imagining my friends' fathers reading bedtime stories while mine was glaringly missing. For years, I quietly cried myself to sleep, believing deep down I was unworthy of love.

This childhood abandonment fractured my ability to build strong relationships and trust others. I often accepted poor treatment from romantic partners and friends because that wounded child inside expected indifference, not devotion. Only through therapy did I trace my lack of boundaries and persistent unworthiness back to the absence of reliable paternal nurturing.

When I finally spoke to my father decades later, his apology unlocked years of hurt. Forgiveness opened the door to self-acceptance that had eluded me since childhood.

Reframe Toxic Messages as Fuel

If you hear the following stories in your self-doubt's voice, it is time to transform pain into purpose:

"You brought this disappointment on yourself."
"You are stupid for dreaming so big."
"You obsess over petty things - something is wrong with you."
"You always make mistakes - you'll never reach your goals."

Our inner critic often echoes childhood traumas. Left unexamined, these hollow voices fuel self-sabotage for decades. Identify and then reframe stories using the laws.

"I am worthy of love and belonging."
"I frame setbacks as helpful feedback to improve."
"Challenges help me clarify and grow."
"My mistakes make me beautifully human, not fatally flawed."

Rewrite limiting stories into fuel for growth and give them less power over you. Suffering becomes strength once reframed.

Cultivating Authentic Confidence

Rejection reveals our true north, guiding us home to our highest selves. Each time criticism or failure forges rather than fractures us, we convert wounds to wisdom, emerging better equipped for the journey ahead. The path to authentic confidence does not come from others' validation. It springs from the well of self-acceptance—an unshakeable certainty in our inherent worth. What if confidence arose from pursuing work that feels meaningful, not seeking applause or approval? This mindset releases us from people-pleasing and performance. Make boldly living your purpose praise enough.

Listen to the whisper inside urging you onward and upward. Let nothing break you, for you were made to persist. Shed perfectionist tendencies. Celebrate small daily progress. Desire propels growth; complacency atrophies dreams. Big goals require big hunger. You contain seeds of greatness awaiting discovery. See yourself succeeding despite current circumstances. The future beckons those willing to believe.

What Rejection Teaches Us

Rejection is inevitable if we dare to put ourselves out there. When rejection strikes, we have a choice: allow it to crush our spirits or use it to strengthen our resolve. Complaining about rejection without learning from it leads nowhere. Each rejection contains a lesson to help us improve. Rather than resent those who reject us, we can be grateful for the feedback to develop our skills further. With an open mindset, rejection polishes our rough edges until we sparkle. We can choose to view rejection as redirection toward our true calling. As we stop taking rejection personally, it loses its sting and power over us. Rejection only has permanence if we permit it. The path forward opens once we close the door on self-pity.

The Power of Perseverance

"Many of life's failures are people who did not realize how close they were to success when they gave up." - **Thomas Edison**

Never Give Up

As we conclude our exploration of the 12 Universal Laws, there is one last crucial principle to emphasize: the importance of perseverance. Simply learning these laws is not enough - you must persist in applying them before you see tangible results. Perseverance means having grit, determination, and the willpower to continue pursuing your dreams despite hardships or repeated setbacks.

This final chapter will highlight incredible stories of perseverance, analyze why you often abandon goals prematurely, and provide tips to help you sustain effort during difficult times on your unique path.

Famous Failures Who Succeeded Through Grit

Some of the most influential figures in history only achieved success after persevering through what seemed like endless disappointments and rejections. Their stories remind you that perseverance pays off in the end if you have the courage not to give up too soon:

FACING REJECTION

Before publishing the first Harry Potter book that would make her a billionaire, J.K. Rowling's original manuscript was rejected by 12 publishers. Steven Spielberg was rejected from film school three times before launching his now legendary career. The Beatles were turned down by multiple record labels who claimed that guitar groups were "on their way out" - but they persisted.

OVERCOMING DISAPPOINTMENTS

Thomas Edison famously conducted 1,000 failed experiments before successfully inventing the lightbulb. Oprah Winfrey was publicly fired from her first television reporting job for being "too emotionally invested" in her stories - but that only drove her to work harder until she became the queen of media.

BEATING THE ODDS

Sylvester Stallone only sold his Rocky script by refusing to give up on it even when he was completely broke and homeless. J.K. Rowling, Steven Spielberg, Thomas Edison, Oprah Winfrey and The Beatles teach you one profound lesson: If you persevere through enough disappointments and rejections, your breakthrough will eventually come.

WHY YOU ABANDON GOALS TOO SOON

If perseverance is so critical for success, why do the majority of people give up on their dreams and goals prematurely? After studying human motivation, psychologists have identified several key reasons:

1. **Unrealistic Timelines:** You underestimate how long meaningful change takes and quit when you don't see immediate results.

2. **Self-Doubt:** Early setbacks or criticism can trigger overwhelming

THE 12 UNIVERSAL LAWS

self-doubt that sabotages your efforts.

3. **Lack of Support Systems:** Without personal and professional support, you lose motivation in isolation.

4. **Impatience with Plateaus:** The path to meaningful goals is never linear - when you hit plateaus, you often quit instead of pushing through.

5. **Prioritizing Comfort:** Stretching towards big goals requires discomfort and sacrifice - too often, you quit because you prioritize short-term comfort over long-term fulfillment.

> **The truth?** Change can often be painfully slow. Obstacles are guaranteed. Critics will always surface. To achieve big goals, perseverance must become a way of life.

STRATEGIES TO PERSEVERE THROUGH ANY STORM

1. **Stay Connected to Your Deeper "Why" Big goals require big effort.** To sustain that effort through every obstacle, continually reconnect to your values, vision and why you embarked on this journey in the first place. Your deeper why gives you strength and courage when nothing else can.

2. **Shift from Outcome-Focused to Process-Focused.** Outcomes like money, fame and status are unreliable motivators. The emotional rollercoaster of "successes" and "failures" burns you out. Instead, focus on daily processes - regardless of external outcomes. Show up fully today. Small daily steps compound over time.

3. **Replace Self-Criticism with Self-Compassion.** Practice talking to yourself the way you would a dear friend in the midst of difficulty. You all suffer from self-doubt, fear, shame and worry as you dare greatly. Counter these draining inner voices with daily

mantras of encouragement.

4. **Celebrate Small Wins.** Meaningful change takes years, not days. Break intimidating goals down into daily progress so that you have frequent opportunities for celebration. Use these quick wins as evidence that you are making progress. Soon, momentum builds.

5. **Stay Accountable to a Supportive Community.** You need others to walk with you when the path feels lonely. Allow trusted mentors, friends and professionals to support you in moments of deep struggle or self-doubt. Use their belief in you to propel yourself forward when your own belief falters.

Perseverance Paves the Road to Success

Legendary journeys always include unexpected twists, turns and false starts. Yours will too. But like J.K. Rowling, Sylvester Stallone, Thomas Edison, and so many others, you will look back one day grateful that you persevered. You will realize perseverance itself paved your road to meaningful success. Stumble, get back up. Lose hope and find it again in those who love you. And never, ever stop moving bravely towards your dreams.

This concludes our journey exploring the 12 Universal Laws. May you now boldly venture out to write the next incredible chapter of your life story - a story certain to inspire generations.

> "What's comin' will come, an' we'll meet it when it does." -**Hagrid**

Epilogue

WE'VE REACHED THE END of our journey exploring the 12 Universal Laws together. I know your mind is swimming with new insights and possibilities. Growth is rarely easy, even when powered by excitement. It's okay to feel a bit unsure - this knowledge is profoundly empowering yet can also feel overwhelming.

What matters most now is how you take these laws from abstract concepts to concrete change. The good news? You already have everything you need within. Will life be perfect now? Of course not. That's the messy beauty of being human. We will stumble and fall. But the laws teach us to get back up again.

There will be setbacks and mistakes ahead. Expect them, but know they are not failures, merely feedback to help you adjust and grow wiser. Reflect on them calmly. Check your alignment with the laws. Then realign and keep manifesting, but remember, just talking about doing something accomplishes nothing. If you want to make something happen, you need to stop discussing it and just take action.

You may doubt yourself at times – that's normal. But your inherent worth was never in question. You were born worthy. Stay centred on that knowledge.

Keep opening doors. You know the way forward now, one step at a time. Manifestation comes through consistency.

You are the author of your story. Write it consciously, write it boldly, write it with love.

Acknowledgments

FIRST AND FOREMOST, I extend my deepest gratitude to those whose wisdom has lit the way. Teachers like Rhonda Byrne, Napoleon Hill, Esther and Jerry Hicks, Jack Canfield, Deepak Chopra, Gabrielle Bernstein, Jen Sincero and Kathryn Zenkina have laid the foundation. I am indebted to all those who walked this path before me. Thank you for shining your light so that others may see more clearly.

To my husband, Ruthven, thank you for being my anchor, my confidant, and my biggest supporter. Your unwavering love and acceptance have allowed me to blossom into the person I am meant to be. I am grateful for the shared laughter, the quiet moments, and the unspoken understanding that binds us. Love you always.

To Mum, Ginny, and JJ whose journey from dark times to the present moment has been a testament to resilience and strength. Each one of you holds a unique place in my heart, and I am immensely proud of the distance we have travelled.

Jayne and Helen, we've weathered so many storms together. Your loyalty and love know no bounds. Thank you both for always having my back. Wendy, your radiant spirit could brighten even the darkest days. Thank you for reminding me that I can do anything.

And to all who have touched my life, even for a moment, "Thank You."

Printed in Great Britain
by Amazon